PUBLISHER'S NOTE

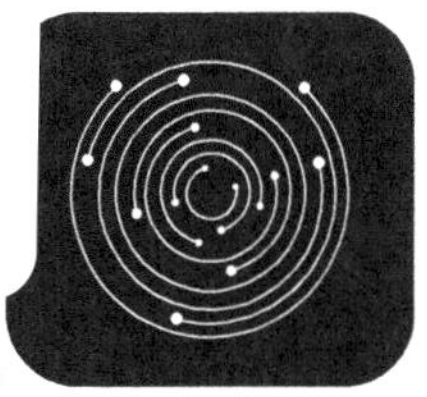

V&S Publishers has carved a significant niche in the publishing industry over the last decade, having successfully published more than 1000 titles across 9 languages spanning over 50 subject categories. Being known for the quality of content, we have built a reputation of excellence and reliability. We have consistently delivered **"Value & Substance"** to our readers, through a wide range of titles across a variety of genres covering school books, fiction and non-fiction that caters to different people from every section of the society.

The **Olympiad Guidebooks for classes 1-10** across all subjects, launched almost a decade ago, under the **GEN X Imprint**, became a go-to-source for the school students in no time, owing to their invaluable and substantive content written in a guidebook pattern,.

Having successfully sold a million copies of the same and in response to demand by both students as well as shopkeepers nationwide; we now present before you our newly launched **Olympiad Workbook Series**, designed for **classes 1-10 across 4 subjects**.

The workbooks are meticulously curated by a team of experienced educators, researchers and subject matter experts, edited by professionals and peer reviewed by teachers. The team has poured its efforts and expertise into creating a crisp and concise workbook which will help and guide the students to the path of success in Olympiad exams. The **MCQs** identified will not only help in scoring top marks in Olympiads but also inculcate a sense of deeper understanding of the subject, by way of solving **HOTS** and referring to complete solutions at the end of the book.

Here we present our new release– **OLYMPIAD WORKBOOK (NSO) CLASS–2** having following features:

- ☞ Based on the latest syllabi
- ☞ MCQs with comprehensive coverage of topics
- ☞ HOTS Questions liberally included
- ☞ A dedicated chapter on logical reasoning
- ☞ Model test paper for thorough practice
- ☞ Sample OMR sheet for real time simulation

We have made sure through our best efforts, that this workbook strictly follows the latest syllabi and patterns of the Olympiad Examination.

As **V&S Publishers** continuously strive to enhance the readability and maintain the credibility of our academic publications, we seek the support of our valuable readers in influencing and enriching the lives of future generations of students.

P.S. While every care has been taken to ensure the correctness of the content, if you come across any error, howsoever minor, do not hesitate to discuss with teachers while pointing that out to us in no uncertain terms.

We wish you all the best for your exams!

DISTINCTIVE FEATURES

01 Learning Objectives

They list the whole chapter as subtopics, helping the teachers to guide children in a step-by-step manner.

02 Multiple Choice Questions

MCQs act as an excellent learning aid, helping you to understand and work on your mistakes.

03 HOTS (Achievers Section)

The High Order Thinking Questions aim to help the student to solve Application-based questions and gain practical understanding of the subject.

04 Model Test Paper

Model test paper are provided at the end of each book, which help the student to test the knowledge which they have gained after thorough reading of all chapters.

05 Answer Key

Detailed Answer Key along with explanations aid the pupil to indentify, understand the mistakes they make during the course of Olympiad preparation.

OLYMPIAD WORKBOOK

NATIONAL SCIENCE OLYMPIAD

01 Learning Objectives

02 Multiple Choice Questions

03 HOTS (Achievers Section)

04 Model Test Paper

05 Answer Keys and Solutions

06 OMR Answer Sheet

V&S PUBLISHERS

Published by:

V&S PUBLISHERS

F-2/16, Ansari road, Daryaganj, New Delhi-110002
☎ 23240026, 23240027 • *Fax:* 011-23240028
✉ info@vspublishers.com • ⊕ www.vspublishers.com

 **Online Brandstore: amazon.in/vspublishers**

Regional Office : Hyderabad
5-1-707/1, Brij Bhawan (Beside Central Bank of India Lane)
Bank Street, Koti, Hyderabad - 500 095
☎ 040-24737290
✉ vspublishershyd@gmail.com

Follow us on:   

BUY OUR BOOKS FROM: AMAZON FLIPKART

© Copyright: V&S PUBLISHERS
ISBN 978-81-977761-8-2
New Edition

DISCLAIMER

While every attempt has been made to provide accurate and timely information in this book, neither the author nor the publisher assumes any responsibility for errors, unintended omissions or commissions detected therein. The author and publisher makes no representation or warranty with respect to the comprehensiveness or completeness of the contents provided.

All matters included have been simplified under professional guidance for general information only, without any warranty for applicability on an individual. Any mention of an organization or a website in the book, by way of citation or as a source of additional information, doesn't imply the endorsement of the content either by the author or the publisher. It is possible that websites cited may have changed or removed between the time of editing and publishing the book.

Results from using the expert opinion in this book will be totally dependent on individual circumstances and factors beyond the control of the author and the publisher.

It makes sense to elicit advice from well informed sources before implementing the ideas given in the book. The reader assumes full responsibility for the consequences arising out from reading this book.

For proper guidance, it is advisable to read the book under the watchful eyes of parents/guardian. The buyer of this book assumes all responsibility for the use of given materials and information.

The copyright of the entire content of this book rests with the author/publisher. Any infringement/transmission of the cover design, text or illustrations, in any form, by any means, by any entity will invite legal action and be responsible for consequences thereon.

CONTENTS

PLANTS

LEARNING OBJECTIVES

➤ Different types of plants and their habitats
➤ Parts of a plant
➤ Uses of plants

MULTIPLE CHOICE QUESTIONS

Direction: Select the correct option for each of the following questions.

1. Very small plants that have soft stems are called _________.
   - (A) Herbs
   - (C) Shrubs
   - (B) Trees
   - (D) Climbers

2. Plant that creep on the ground ______.
   - (A) Jackfruit
   - (B) Watermelon
   - (C) Rose
   - (D) Pineapple

3. A tree stem is protected by an outer covering called _________.
   - (A) Branch
   - (B) Cork
   - (C) Bark
   - (D) Trunk

4. Brinjal plant is a _________.
   - (A) Herb
   - (B) Shrub
   - (C) Tree
   - (D) None of these

5. Which of these plant live for only one season?
   - (A) Mango
   - (B) Guava
   - (C) Rubber plant
   - (D) Rice

Directions (6 – 8): Based on the image given below, answer the questions.

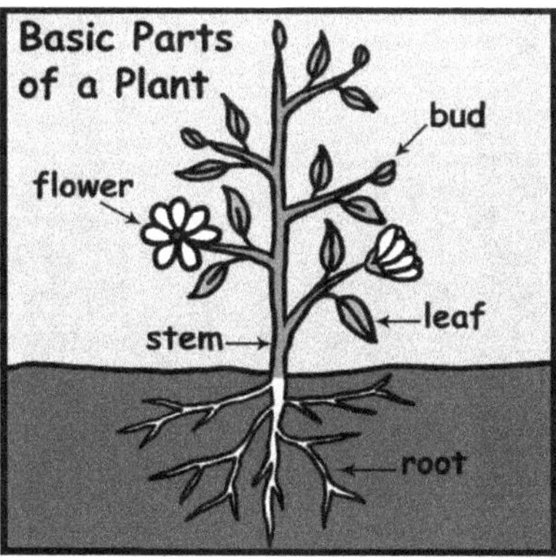

6. Which part of the plant helps in transpiration?
   - (A) Stem
   - (B) Leaves
   - (C) Roots
   - (D) Branches

7. Which part of a plant helps in photosynthesis or the production of sugar and release of oxygen?
   - (A) Roots
   - (B) Flowers
   - (C) Stem
   - (D) Leaves

8. Which part of a plant helps in transporting the nutrients from the soil?
   - (A) Roots
   - (B) Flowers
   - (C) Stem
   - (D) Leaves

9. The correct order of a plant's life cycle is __________.
   (A) Seed, sprout, seedling, plant, and flower
   (B) Sprout, seed, seedling, plant, and flower
   (C) Flower, seed, seedling, sprout, and plant
   (D) Flower, seed, seedling, and sprout

10. Cactus plants are part of which of the following plant categories?
    (A) Aquatic plants
    (B) Coniferous plants
    (C) Deciduous plants
    (D) Desert plants

11. Which is the odd plant among the following?

(A)   (B)
(C)   (D)

12. Which of these is not a desert plant feature?
    (A) Spines
    (B) No leaves
    (C) Thick spongy stem
    (D) Lots of flowers

13. Plant that grow on land are called __________.
    (A) Aquatic plants
    (B) Coniferous plants
    (C) Terrestrial plants
    (D) Xerophytes

14. Floating and fixed plants are a variety of __________.
    (A) Aquatic plants
    (B) Coniferous plants
    (C) Terrestrial plants
    (D) Xerophytes

15. Trees on plains do not have which of these characteristics?
    (A) Autumn shedding of leaves
    (B) Lots of stomata
    (C) Lots of leaves
    (D) Adapted to high heat and dry conditions

16. Which of these is not a thorny plant?
    (A) Jackfruit
    (B) Lemon
    (C) Bougainvillea
    (D) Prickly pear

17. Thorns of which of these plants are actually reduced leaves?
    (A) Rose   (B) Lemon
    (C) Bougainvillea (D) Prickly pear

18. Broad, waxy leaves are found in __________.
    (A) Cactus   (B) Banyan
    (C) Hibiscus   (D) Water lily

19. Which of the following plants correctly matches the given description?
    I am a small plant.
    I have a number of roots growing from the base of my stem.
    I am seasonal.
    (A) Wheat   (C) Carrot
    (B) Mango tree   (D) Rose

20. Raghu is classifying some vegetables according to the part of the plant that we eat. He has done a mistake. Which vegetable is wrongly classified?

Vegetable	Part of Plant
Carrot	Stem
Cabbage	Leaves
Potato	Flower
Cauliflower	Flower
Beetroot	Root
Onion	Leaves
Brinjal	Fruit

(A) Brinjal
(B) Onion and potato
(C) Cabbage
(D) Carrot

21. Kartik was confused when his father asked him which plant fibre is stuffed in his pillow. Help him name it.
    (A) Jute   (B) Coconut
    (C) Wool   (D) Cotton

22. What are the similarities between the two plants given below?

    (A) They both have thick, woody stems
    (B) They are creepers
    (C) They are herbs
    (D) They have weak, soft stems

23. Ravi planted two plants in two pots. Plant A had no roots while plant B had no leaves. Which plant will die?
    (A) Plant A and B both will die because they do not have roots and leaves, respectively
    (B) Plant A will die because roots are important to take up nutrition from soil and helps in plant growth
    (C) Plant B will die because leaves are important for making food
    (D) Nor plant A neither plant B will die

24. Which of the following is important for a plant?

    (A)   (B)
    (C)   (D)

25. Oil is not obtained from which of the following plant?
    (A) Mango plant
    (B) Sunflower plant
    (C) Mustard plant
    (D) Coconut plant

HOTS (ACHIEVERS SECTION)

26. The photograph below shows a cactus plant covered with sharp spines.
    What are the spines for?

    (A) They lose almost no water at all
    (B) They provide support to the plant
    (C) They attract bees
    (D) They carry food to the flower

27. Identify one example of the following and select the correct option.
    i. Plant 'G' lives for many years and plant 'I' has a weak stem.
    ii. Plant 'H' grows in water and plant 'J' grows on mountains and hills.

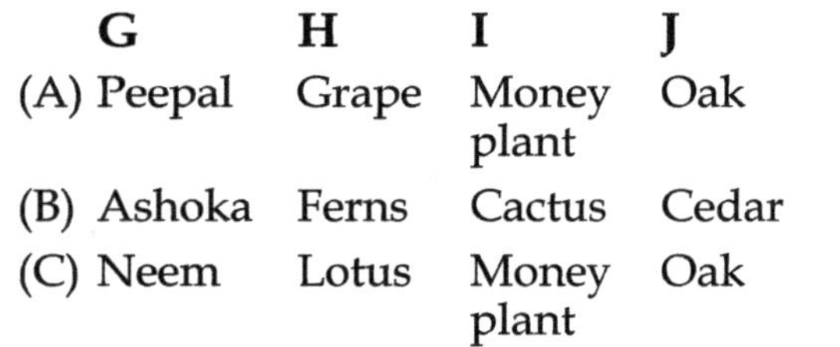

	G	**H**	**I**	**J**
(A)	Peepal	Grape	Money plant	Oak
(B)	Ashoka	Ferns	Cactus	Cedar
(C)	Neem	Lotus	Money plant	Oak
(D)	Mango	Grape	Ferns	Ashoka

28. Which of the following statement is true for a herb?
    (A) Herb are small plants
    (B) Herb has soft stem
    (C) Herb needs the support of other plants to grow
    (D) Both (A) and (B)

29. Study the given flowchart and select the option to correctly fill the empty space x and y.

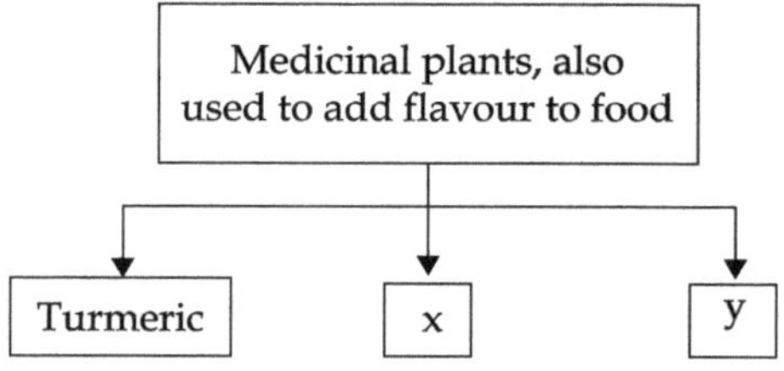

    (A) Mint and clove
    (B) Clove and Neam
    (C) Tulsi and Cocoa
    (D) Cardamon and Almond

30. Plants give us food grains. What are the examples of such grains?
    (A) Wheat and Rice
    (B) Maize and Barley
    (C) Gram and Pulses
    (D) All of these

1.	Ⓐ Ⓑ Ⓒ Ⓓ	7.	Ⓐ Ⓑ Ⓒ Ⓓ	13.	Ⓐ Ⓑ Ⓒ Ⓓ	19	Ⓐ Ⓑ Ⓒ Ⓓ	25.	Ⓐ Ⓑ Ⓒ Ⓓ
2.	Ⓐ Ⓑ Ⓒ Ⓓ	8.	Ⓐ Ⓑ Ⓒ Ⓓ	14.	Ⓐ Ⓑ Ⓒ Ⓓ	20.	Ⓐ Ⓑ Ⓒ Ⓓ	26.	Ⓐ Ⓑ Ⓒ Ⓓ
3.	Ⓐ Ⓑ Ⓒ Ⓓ	9.	Ⓐ Ⓑ Ⓒ Ⓓ	15.	Ⓐ Ⓑ Ⓒ Ⓓ	21.	Ⓐ Ⓑ Ⓒ Ⓓ	27.	Ⓐ Ⓑ Ⓒ Ⓓ
4.	Ⓐ Ⓑ Ⓒ Ⓓ	10.	Ⓐ Ⓑ Ⓒ Ⓓ	16.	Ⓐ Ⓑ Ⓒ Ⓓ	22.	Ⓐ Ⓑ Ⓒ Ⓓ	28.	Ⓐ Ⓑ Ⓒ Ⓓ
5.	Ⓐ Ⓑ Ⓒ Ⓓ	11.	Ⓐ Ⓑ Ⓒ Ⓓ	17.	Ⓐ Ⓑ Ⓒ Ⓓ	23.	Ⓐ Ⓑ Ⓒ Ⓓ	29.	Ⓐ Ⓑ Ⓒ Ⓓ
6.	Ⓐ Ⓑ Ⓒ Ⓓ	12.	Ⓐ Ⓑ Ⓒ Ⓓ	18.	Ⓐ Ⓑ Ⓒ Ⓓ	24.	Ⓐ Ⓑ Ⓒ Ⓓ	30.	Ⓐ Ⓑ Ⓒ Ⓓ

ANIMALS

LEARNING OBJECTIVES

- ➤ Types of plants
- ➤ Where do plants come from?
- ➤ Parts of a plant
- ➤ Sources of food

MULTIPLE CHOICE QUESTIONS

Direction: Select the correct option for each of the following questions.

1. Which of these kill other animals for food?

(A)   (B)   (C)    (D) 

2. Which of these help to keep the jungles clean by eating dead animals?

(A)   (B)    (C)    (D) 

3. Which of these wild animals are herbivores?
   (A) Elephants   (B) Black bear
   (C) Monkeys   (D) All of them

4. Who am I?
   I am a big animal with big ears and a trunk. I love to eat sugarcane.
   (A) Herbivore   (B) Plant eater
   (C) Carnivore   (D) Both (A) and (B)

5. To help keep unwanted animals away from your home __________.
   (A) Leave bowls of pet food on the doorway
   (B) Keep garbage in tightly covered garbage cans
   (C) Keep water in buckets nearby
   (D) None of these

6. If you are bitten or scratched by an animal, you should __________.
   (A) Wash the wound with lots of soap and water
   (B) Tell an adult
   (C) Chase the animal
   (D) Both (A) and (B)

7. Animals that most often get rabies are __________.
   (A) Cats   (B) Dogs
   (C) Monkeys   (D) Lizards

8. Which of these animals gives us leather?
   (A) Snake   (B) Ant
   (C) Fish   (D) Sheep

9. Which of these animals gives us honey?
   (A) Housefly   (B) Bee
   (C) Mosquito   (D) Butterfly

10. Which of the following statements is correct?
    (A) Some animals have sharp front teeth both in upper and lower jaws to break open fruits and nuts
    (B) Grass-eating animals have strong broad back teeth to grind their food
    (C) Flesh-eating animals have pointed teeth to tear flesh
    (D) All of these statements are correct

11. Which of these is a wrong match?
    (A) Crows-caw   (B) Cows-bark
    (C) Cats-meow   (D) Sparrows-chirp

12. In the given image, who is the herbivore?

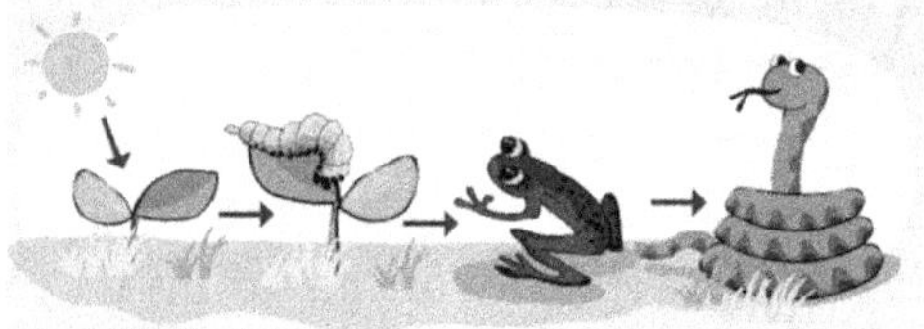

    (A) Frog   (B) Snake
    (C) Caterpillar   (D) None of them

13. In the given image, who is the most important?

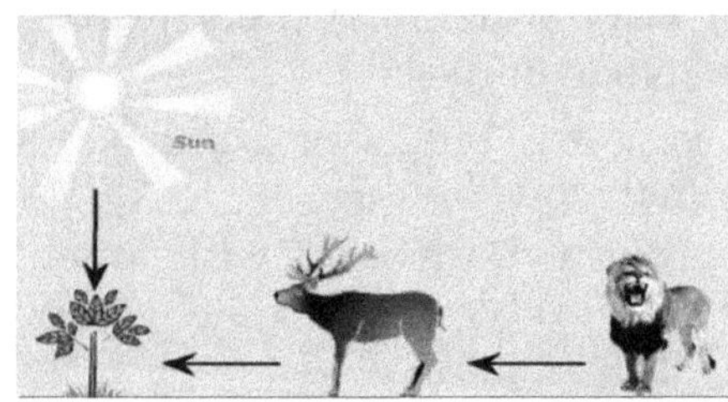

    (A) Deer   (B) Lion
    (C) Plant   (D) All of these

14. Which of the following lay eggs?

(A)    (B) 

(C)    (D) 

15. We get _______ from animals.

(A)    (B) 

(C) 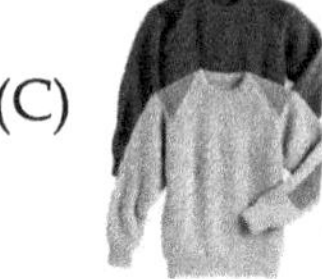   (D) Both (A) and (C)

16. Which of the following have webbed feet?

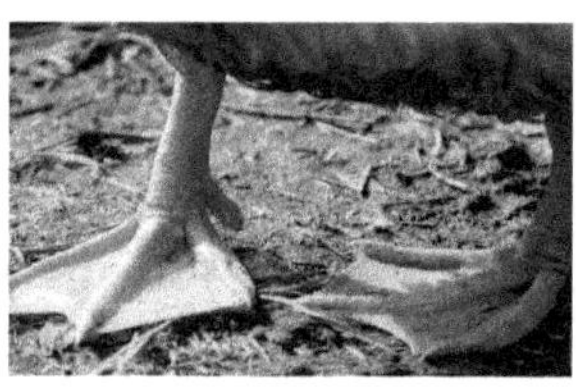

    (A) Elephants   (B) Snake
    (C) Ducks   (D) Sparrow

17. An animal lives in water, eats other animals, and gives birth to babies in water. Who is this animal?
    (A) Shark   (B) Whale
    (C) Dolphin   (D) Crocodile

18. Which animal's offspring is called a "calf"?
    (A) Dog   (B) Cow
    (C) Bear   (D) Duck

19. Deer are eaten by _______.
    (A) Herbivores   (B) Carnivores
    (C) Omnivores   (D) Both (B) and (C)

20. What is common among the following animals?

OLYMPIAD WORKBOOK (NSO) CLASS–2

(A) They lay eggs and have wings
(B) They have wings
(C) They lay eggs
(D) They are carnivores

21. What is common among the following animals?

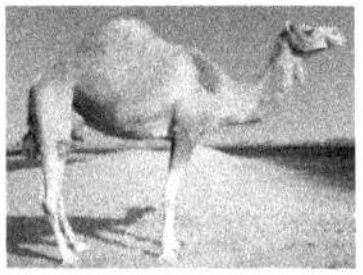

(A) They give us useful products like milk
(B) They are farm animals
(C) They can be tamed
(D) All of these

22. Which is the correct match?

I	II
A. Buffalo	i. Egg giving animal
B. Goat	ii. Meat giving animal
C. Lion	iii. Milk giving domestic animal
D. Hen	iv. Wild carnivore

(A) A (iii), B (ii), C (iv), D (i)
(B) A (ii), B (iii), C (i), D (iv)
(C) A (i), B (ii), C (iv), D (iii)
(D) A (iii), B (i), C (iv), D (ii)

23. Read the poem below and find out what is wrong.

Monkeys can jump and climb trees,
Giraffes are short and they eat leaves.
Parrots are colourful and they can fly,
Elephants can't but would love to try.
Turtles are green and they can swim,
Cheetahs can run and they always win.
Zebras look like horses but they are black and white,
Hippos are big and snore at night.

(A) Turtles cannot swim
(B) Zebras resemble cows
(C) Giraffes are not short
(D) Parrots are not colourful

24. White tigers are ________.
(A) Extinct
(B) Endangered
(C) Protected
(D) Endangered and threatened

25. Identify the bird given in the picture below. Name the country whose national animal this bird is ________.

(A) Kiwi, Australia
(B) Kiwi, New Zealand
(C) Penguin, Australia
(D) Kiwi, America

HOTS (ACHIEVERS SECTION)

26. Select the correct option from column I and column II.

I. A black bear eats different things, such as grasses, roots, and berries. It also eats insects, fish, and other small animals. Which of these BEST describes a black bear?

II. A wolf eats deer, bison, moose, etc. Which of these BEST describes a wolf?

	I	II
(A)	Omnivore	Carnivore
(B)	Herbivore	Carnivore
(C)	Omnivore	Omnivore
(D)	Producer	Carnivore

27. Study the given flowchart. Identify one example of the following and select the correct option.

i. Animal 'G' eats the flesh of dead animals and animal 'I' gives honey.

ii. Animal 'H' is a scavenger and animal 'J' is used for riding.

	G	H	I	J
(A)	Jackal	Hen	Sheep	Goat
(B)	Crocodile	Hyenas	Honeybee	Horse
(C)	Vulture	Sheep	Snake	Camel
(D)	Hyena	Horse	Giraffe	Chicken

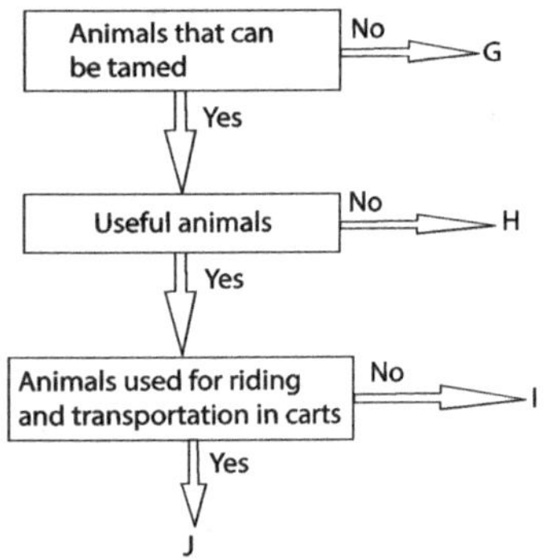

28. Match column I with column II and select the correct option.

I	II
A. Ship of the desert	1. Elephant
B. Ship of Himalayan region	2. Reindeer
C. Animal as transport in South-east Asia	3. Camel
D. Animal as transport in Arctic and sub-Arctic Nordic	4. Yak

(A) A-3; B-4; C-1; D-2
(B) A-3; B-2; C-1; D-4
(C) A-1; B-2; C-4; D-3
(D) A-1; B-3; C-4; D-2

29. The following are the list of animals and foods obtained from them. Match List I with List II.

	List I		List II
A.	Hen	1.	Bird
B.	Cow	2.	Insect
C.	Camel	3.	Lives in desert
D.	Butterfly	4.	Domestic animal

(A) A-2 B-3 C-4 D-1
(B) A-1 B-2 C-4 D-3
(C) A-1 B-4 C-3 D-2
(D) A-2 B-3 C-4 D-1

30. Group 1: Lion, bear, tiger, elephant
Group 2: Ox, cow, horse

Which of the following is correct about the given groups of animals?

(A) Group 1: Domestic animals, Group 2: Wild animals
(B) Group 1: Wild animals, Group 2: Domestic animals
(C) Both Group 1 and Group 2 have Domestic animal
(D) None of these

Darken Your Choice with HB Pencil

1.	A B C D	7.	A B C D	13.	A B C D	19	A B C D	25.	A B C D
2.	A B C D	8.	A B C D	14.	A B C D	20.	A B C D	26.	A B C D
3.	A B C D	9.	A B C D	15.	A B C D	21.	A B C D	27.	A B C D
4.	A B C D	10.	A B C D	16.	A B C D	22.	A B C D	28.	A B C D
5.	A B C D	11.	A B C D	17.	A B C D	23.	A B C D	29.	A B C D
6.	A B C D	12.	A B C D	18.	A B C D	24.	A B C D	30.	A B C D

HUMAN BODY

LEARNING OBJECTIVES

➤ External body organs
➤ Internal body organs
➤ How to keep bones and muscles healthy

➤ Sensory organs
➤ Bones and muscles of body

MULTIPLE CHOICE QUESTIONS

Direction: Select the correct option for each of the following questions.

1. The limbs which help us to hold something are called __________.
   (A) Arms   (B) Toes
   (C) Hands   (D) Legs

2. Which is the largest sensory organ of human body?
   (A) Ears   (B) Skin
   (C) Tongue   (D) Eyes

3. Which organ helps to maintain our body temperature?
   (A) Ears   (B) Skin
   (C) Tongue   (D) Eyes

4. The body parts which can be seen are called __________.
   (A) External organs
   (B) Internal organs
   (C) Spare organs
   (D) Mobile organs

5. The body parts which are functioning internally and cannot be seen outside are called __________.
   (A) Internal organs
   (B) External organs
   (C) Extreme organs
   (D) Intertwined organs

6. The organ which gives shape to our body is called the __________.
   (A) Skeleton   (B) Skin
   (C) Heart   (D) Lungs

7. Which is the organ that filters the blood and releases waste substance in the form of urine?
   (A) Kidneys   (B) Skin
   (C) Heart   (D) Lungs

8. Brain is protected by a hard bony cover called the __________.
   (A) Skeleton   (B) Skull
   (C) Rib cage   (D) Skin

9. Lungs are protected by the __________.
   (A) Skeleton   (B) Skull
   (C) Rib cage   (D) Skin

10. The master organ of our body is the __________.
    (A) Heart   (B) Lungs
    (C) Stomach   (D) Brain

11. Eye is the sense of organ for __________.
    (A) Smell   (B) Hearing
    (C) Vision   (D) Touch

12. You hear sounds through __________.
    (A) Vibration   (B) Music
    (C) Noise   (D) Light

13. Your _________ are groups of cells inside your mouth that detect the taste of the food you eat.
    (A) Tongue
    (B) Teeth
    (C) Taste buds
    (D) Saliva

14. Which sense do you use to detect which perfume has good odour?
    (A) Taste
    (B) Smell
    (C) Sight
    (D) Touch

15. Which body parts are used by the girl in the picture?

    (A) Only legs
    (B) Only hands
    (C) Facial expressions
    (D) Whole body

16. Hearing disability may happen due to _________.
    (A) Loud noise
    (B) Loud music
    (C) Sound of crackers
    (D) All of these

17. In which of the following activities do we use our body the least _________.
    (A) Sleeping
    (B) Jumping
    (C) Singing
    (D) Eating

18. Which of the following statements is correct?
    (A) Our bones are covered with muscles
    (B) Muscles help us move
    (C) There are more than 600 muscles in our body
    (D) All of these

19. The place where two or more bones are joined are called _________.
    (A) Muscles
    (B) Tendon
    (C) Joint
    (D) Elbows

20. In the following, whose heart will beat the fastest?
    (A) Neha is sitting
    (B) Rohan is running
    (C) Preeti is standing
    (D) Gauri is reading

21. The role of the organ given below is _________.

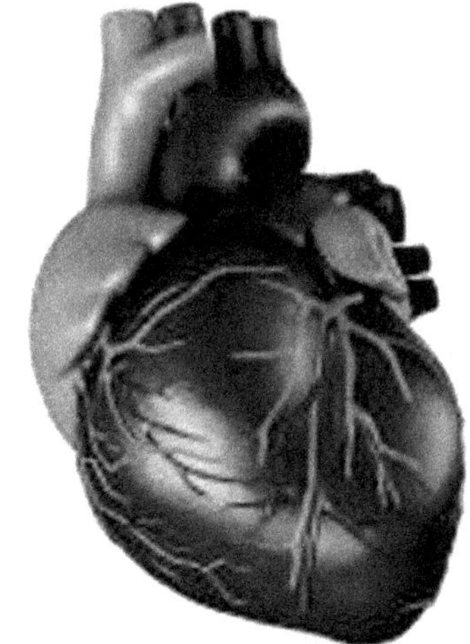

    (A) Pump blood   (B) Think and act
    (C) Taste food   (D) Excrete waste

22. Good posture keeps our back pain free. Which of the following is not a good posture?

OLYMPIAD WORKBOOK (NSO) CLASS−2

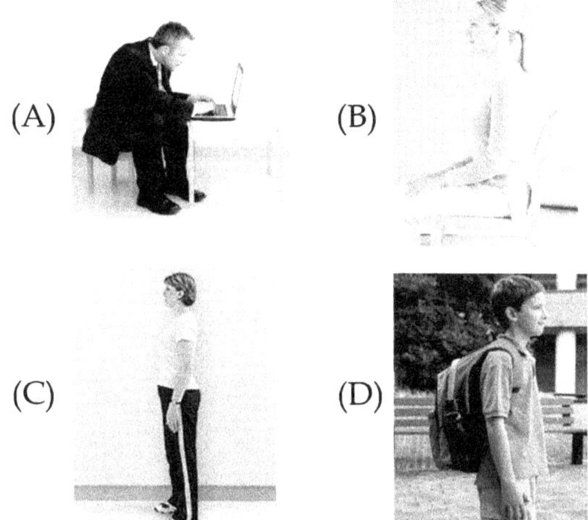

23. Which part of the body can we bend?
(A) Knee   (B) Elbow
(C) Both (A) and (B)   (D) Rib cage

24. Which of the following is not a sensory organ?
(A) Stomach   (B) Tongue
(C) Finger tips   (D) Eyes

25. Identify this joint __________.

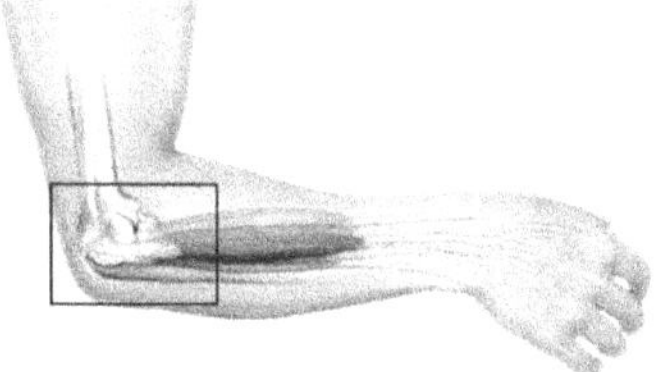

(A) Knee   (B) Elbow
(C) Hip   (D) Shoulder

HOTS (ACHIEVERS SECTION)

26. The diagram below shows the digestive system of the human body.

The part marked __________ removes water from the undigested food.

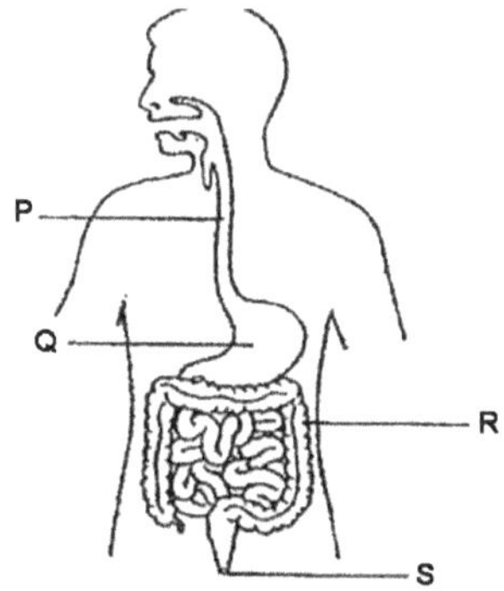

(A) P   (B) S
(C) R   (D) Q

27. Trisha: Eyes are the external part of our body.

Rita: Every human beings have two eyes.
Which of these statements are true?

(A) Trisha only
(B) Rita only
(C) Both Trisha and Rita
(D) None of these

28. Which of the following is false about human nose?
(A) Nose is located in the internal part of the head
(B) Nose helps us to breathe
(C) Nose helps us to smell
(D) Nose has two holes

29. Ritu: Our bones are covered with muscles.

Ananya: Muscles help us to move our bones.

(A) Both Ritu and Ananya are true
(B) Only Ritu
(C) Only Ananya
(D) None of these

30. Which of the following is true about skin?

    i.   Skin is the internal part of the body.

    ii.   It is a sense organ because it gives us the sense of taste.

    iii.   Skin covers the whole body.

    iv.   Skin can be white, black or wheatish is colour.

(A) Both (i) and (ii)

(B) Both (iii) and (iv)

(C) Both (ii) and (iii)

(D) All are true

——————————Darken Your Choice with HB Pencil——————————

1.	Ⓐ Ⓑ Ⓒ Ⓓ	7.	Ⓐ Ⓑ Ⓒ Ⓓ	13.	Ⓐ Ⓑ Ⓒ Ⓓ	19	Ⓐ Ⓑ Ⓒ Ⓓ	25.	Ⓐ Ⓑ Ⓒ Ⓓ
2.	Ⓐ Ⓑ Ⓒ Ⓓ	8.	Ⓐ Ⓑ Ⓒ Ⓓ	14.	Ⓐ Ⓑ Ⓒ Ⓓ	20.	Ⓐ Ⓑ Ⓒ Ⓓ	26.	Ⓐ Ⓑ Ⓒ Ⓓ
3.	Ⓐ Ⓑ Ⓒ Ⓓ	9.	Ⓐ Ⓑ Ⓒ Ⓓ	15.	Ⓐ Ⓑ Ⓒ Ⓓ	21.	Ⓐ Ⓑ Ⓒ Ⓓ	27.	Ⓐ Ⓑ Ⓒ Ⓓ
4.	Ⓐ Ⓑ Ⓒ Ⓓ	10.	Ⓐ Ⓑ Ⓒ Ⓓ	16.	Ⓐ Ⓑ Ⓒ Ⓓ	22.	Ⓐ Ⓑ Ⓒ Ⓓ	28.	Ⓐ Ⓑ Ⓒ Ⓓ
5.	Ⓐ Ⓑ Ⓒ Ⓓ	11.	Ⓐ Ⓑ Ⓒ Ⓓ	17.	Ⓐ Ⓑ Ⓒ Ⓓ	23.	Ⓐ Ⓑ Ⓒ Ⓓ	29.	Ⓐ Ⓑ Ⓒ Ⓓ
6.	Ⓐ Ⓑ Ⓒ Ⓓ	12.	Ⓐ Ⓑ Ⓒ Ⓓ	18.	Ⓐ Ⓑ Ⓒ Ⓓ	24.	Ⓐ Ⓑ Ⓒ Ⓓ	30.	Ⓐ Ⓑ Ⓒ Ⓓ

FOOD

LEARNING OBJECTIVES

- ➤ Our sense organs
- ➤ Good habits
- ➤ Clothes
- ➤ Balanced food
- ➤ Shelter

MULTIPLE CHOICE QUESTIONS

Direction: Select the correct option for each of the following questions.

1. Which of these food items helps us to grow?

(A) 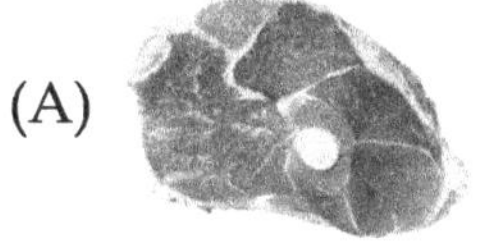

(B) 

(C) 

(D) 

2. Which food is categorized as protective food?

(A) 

(B) 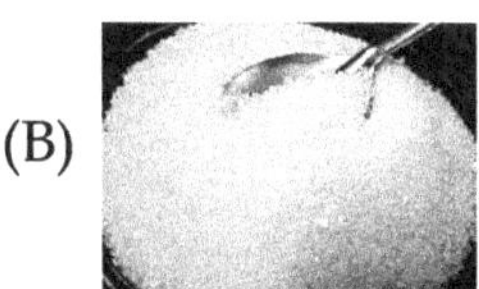

(C) 

(D) 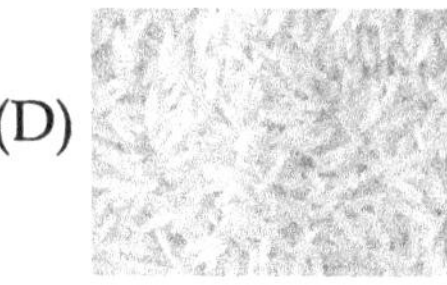

3. Which food item is a rich source of carbohydrates?
   (A) Cauliflower (B) Fish
   (C) Rice (D) Eggs

4. To be able to do more work, we need __________.
   (A) Energy (B) Vitamins
   (C) Water (D) Protein

5. What will happen if we do not eat proteins?
   (A) We will not have energy to work.
   (B) We will not grow well.
   (C) We will become healthy.
   (D) We will become weak and not grow well.

6. Which category includes sugarcane?
   (A) Energy giving (B) Body building
   (C) Protective (D) Both (B) and (C)

7. Which is the richest source of good-quality protein?
   (A) Pulses (B) Cereals
   (C) Egg (D) Meat

8. Iron is a __________.
   (A) Carbohydrate (B) Mineral
   (C) Protein (D) Vitamin

9. Fruits are rich in __________.
   (A) Minerals
   (B) Proteins
   (C) Vitamins and minerals
   (D) Carbohydrates

10. If you need to replace milk in your diet, you should choose which of the following?
    (A) Cereals
    (B) Leafy vegetables
    (C) Pulses
    (D) Cheeses

11. For good-quality protein, which of the following should be your choice?
    (A) Apples (B) Eggs
    (C) Spinach (D) Cabbage

12. Which of the following foods have all the essential nutrients?
    (A) Butter (B) Eggs
    (C) Meat (D) Pulses

13. Potatoes are a rich source of ________.
    (A) Body-building materials
    (B) Energy-providing materials
    (C) Protective materials
    (D) All nutrients

14. A food item that provides only energy is ________.
    (A) Bajra (B) Rice
    (C) Sugar (D) Wheat

15. Spices help to make food taste good. Which of these is not a spice?
    (A) Raisin (B) Cinnamon
    (C) Turmeric (D) Chillies

16. Which of these minerals make our bone strong?
    (A) Calcium (B) Iron
    (C) Chlorine (D) Sodium

17. Which of the following is a bad habit?
    (A) Eating a variety of food items
    (B) Exercising regularly
    (C) Swallowing the food without chewing
    (D) Drinking a lot of water

18. Fats and carbohydrates are together called ________.
    (A) Protective foods
    (B) Body-building food
    (C) Junk food
    (D) Energy giving food

19. Sahil should not eat which of the following?

(A) (B)

(C) (D)

20. We should not skip this meal because the body requires it the most after hours of gap between meals. Which meal are we referring to?
    (A) Dinner (B) Lunch
    (C) Breakfast (D) Supper

21. Why is fish kept in ice as shown in the given image?

    (A) It tastes good.
    (B) It cooks well.
    (C) It stays fresh for a longer time.
    (D) Its nutritional value is increased.

22. Select the odd one out.
    (A) Walnut (B) Raisin
    (C) Grapes (D) Almonds

23. Rice is mostly eaten in southern and eastern India. It is termed as ________.
    (A) Staple food
    (B) Balanced food
    (C) Junk food
    (D) Breakfast food

24. We should have one energy-giving food, one protective food, and one body-building food in every meal. Which combination out of the following options is the best?
   (A) Rice, dal, and curd
   (B) Soup and bread sticks
   (C) Rice, dal, and paneer
   (D) Chapati, dal, vegetables, and curd

25. Which of these is used to make a beverage?

(A)    (B) 

(C)    (D) Both (B) and (C)

HOTS (ACHIEVERS SECTION)

26. Different kinds of food help us in different ways. Some foods give us energy. Some foods help us grow and some foods keep us healthy.

   I. The food items shown in the given pictures fall under which food group?
   II. Which of them is not an animal food product?

	I	II
(A)	Protective foods	Eggs
(B)	Body building food	Pulses
(C)	Roughage-giving food	Milk
(D)	Energy-giving food	Pulses

27. Find which of the following is under wrong heading?

Body-building food	Protective food	Energy giving food
Milk	Fish	Sugar
Meat	Fruits	Cashew nuts

   (A) Milk   (B) Cashew nut
   (C) Fish   (D) Fruits

28. Read the following sentences and identify the food item.
   A. I am a complete food.
   B. I help you to grow and give you energy.
   C. I protect you from diseases.
   D. A small baby drinks only me Guess who I am?
   (A) Egg   (B) Pumpkin
   (C) Milk   (D) Meat

29. Consider the following statements and find true and false (T/F).
   A. We should eat only meat to remain healthy.
   B. Eating vegetables makes us ill.
   C. A small baby drinks only milk.
   (A) TTT   (B) FFT
   (C) TFT   (D) FFF

30. Match the following:

A	Orange	1	River
B	Sugar	2	Cow
C	Milk	3	Sugarcane
D	Fish	4	Plant

(A) A-1, B-3, C-2, D-4
(B) A-4, B-3, C-2, D-1
(C) A-2, B-3, C-4, D-1
(D) A-1, B-2, C-3, D-4

1.	Ⓐ Ⓑ Ⓒ Ⓓ	7.	Ⓐ Ⓑ Ⓒ Ⓓ	13.	Ⓐ Ⓑ Ⓒ Ⓓ	19.	Ⓐ Ⓑ Ⓒ Ⓓ	25.	Ⓐ Ⓑ Ⓒ Ⓓ
2.	Ⓐ Ⓑ Ⓒ Ⓓ	8.	Ⓐ Ⓑ Ⓒ Ⓓ	14.	Ⓐ Ⓑ Ⓒ Ⓓ	20.	Ⓐ Ⓑ Ⓒ Ⓓ	26.	Ⓐ Ⓑ Ⓒ Ⓓ
3.	Ⓐ Ⓑ Ⓒ Ⓓ	9.	Ⓐ Ⓑ Ⓒ Ⓓ	15.	Ⓐ Ⓑ Ⓒ Ⓓ	21.	Ⓐ Ⓑ Ⓒ Ⓓ	27.	Ⓐ Ⓑ Ⓒ Ⓓ
4.	Ⓐ Ⓑ Ⓒ Ⓓ	10.	Ⓐ Ⓑ Ⓒ Ⓓ	16.	Ⓐ Ⓑ Ⓒ Ⓓ	22.	Ⓐ Ⓑ Ⓒ Ⓓ	28.	Ⓐ Ⓑ Ⓒ Ⓓ
5.	Ⓐ Ⓑ Ⓒ Ⓓ	11.	Ⓐ Ⓑ Ⓒ Ⓓ	17.	Ⓐ Ⓑ Ⓒ Ⓓ	23.	Ⓐ Ⓑ Ⓒ Ⓓ	29.	Ⓐ Ⓑ Ⓒ Ⓓ
6.	Ⓐ Ⓑ Ⓒ Ⓓ	12.	Ⓐ Ⓑ Ⓒ Ⓓ	18.	Ⓐ Ⓑ Ⓒ Ⓓ	24.	Ⓐ Ⓑ Ⓒ Ⓓ	30.	Ⓐ Ⓑ Ⓒ Ⓓ

OLYMPIAD WORKBOOK (NSO) CLASS–2

HOUSING AND CLOTHING 

LEARNING OBJECTIVES

- ➤ Types of houses
- ➤ Building material
- ➤ Different kinds of roofs
- ➤ How are clothes made?

MULTIPLE CHOICE QUESTIONS

Direction: Select the correct option for each of the following questions.

1. Which of the following is a permanent house?
   (A) Igloo　　　　　(B) Tent
   (C) Bungalow　　　(D) Caravans

2. Which of the following people use temporary houses?
   (A) Soldiers　　　　(B) Scouts
   (C) Mountaineers　(D) All of these

3. In Kashmir, tourists like to stay in __________.
   (A) Caravans　　　(B) Houseboats
   (C) Igloos　　　　(D) None of these

4. One would find a houseboat in __________.
   (A) Rajasthan　　　(B) Uttarakhand
   (C) Kashmir　　　　(D) Mumbai

5. When we need to go out in the rain, we should take an umbrella or wear a __________.
   (A) Sweater　　　　(B) Raincoat
   (C) Scarf　　　　　(D) Kurta

6. Which of the following houses have roof made of straw or palm leaves?
   (A) Tent houses　　(B) Caravans
   (C) Igloos　　　　(D) Mud houses

7. Why do houses have sloping roofs?
   (A) To absorb water
   (B) To absorb heat
   (C) To look beautiful
   (D) To help the rain water and snow slip off easily

8. Houses in the plains have __________.
   (A) Semi-circular roofs
   (B) Curved roofs
   (C) Flat roofs
   (D) Sloping roofs

9. Mountain climbers often carry __________.
   (A) Blocks　　　　(B) Tents
   (C) Cardboards　　(D) Asbestos sheets

10. Pucca or permanent houses are built with __________.
    (A) Bricks, stones, and cement
    (B) Cement, grass, and iron rods
    (C) Bricks, grass, and water
    (D) Stones, cement, and iron rods

11. Kutcha or temporary houses are built with __________.
    (A) Bricks, stones, and cement
    (B) Mud, grass, and waste material
    (C) Bricks, grass, and water
    (D) Stones, cement, and iron rods

12. The following image shows a house which is built in those places where _________.

(A) Wind blows very fast.
(B) It rains heavily.
(C) Climatic conditions are very cold.
(D) Heat of the Sun is extreme.

13. It is important to put a wire mesh on doors and windows because _________.
(A) It keeps the house warm and dark.
(B) It allows sunlight and air to come in.
(C) It stops the entry of mosquitoes and flies.
(D) Both (B) and (C)

14. Which of these kinds of houses are famous in Japan?
(A) Built of paper
(B) Built of wood
(C) Built of wood and paper
(D) Built of cement

15. Which of the following gives fibres used to make a sweater?
(A) Sheep
(B) Cocoon
(C) Deer
(D) Plants

16. Which of the following gives fibres used to make a silk sari?
(A) Sheep
(B) Silk worm
(C) Deer
(D) Plants

17. Clothes are made from _________.
(A) Worms
(B) Plants
(C) Animals
(D) Fibres

18. We wear different clothes. This depends on _________.
(A) Type of season
(B) Type of climate
(C) Type of occasion
(D) All of these

19. We wear cotton clothes mostly in _________.
(A) Rainy season
(B) Winter season
(C) Summer season
(D) None of these

20. Which of the following will least absorb sweat?
(A) Cotton clothes
(B) Nylon socks
(C) Silk sari
(D) Sweaters

21. On a sunny day, when we spread wet clothes on a clothesline for drying under the Sun, the following observing points can be extracted _________.
Which of the following statements is/are correct?
(A) Silk clothes absorb the most water.
(B) Cotton clothes are heaviest among other fabric clothes.
(C) Woollen clothes take the longest time to dry.
(D) Both (A) and (B)

22. A raincoat is made up of _________.
(A) Plastic
(B) A fabric that repels water
(C) A fabric that is water proof
(D) All of these

23. Select the incorrect statement from the statements given below.
(A) Woollen clothes keep us warm.
(B) Woollen clothes absorb sweat from our body.
(C) Cotton clothes keeps us cool.
(D) Synthetic clothes are good to wear in winters.

24. Woollen clothes are made by which process?
(A) Weaving
(B) Wearing
(C) Knitting
(D) Spinning

25. Gandhi ji used to wear _________.
(A) Cotton clothes
(B) Khadi clothes
(C) Synthetic clothes
(D) Silk clothes

26. Match column I with column II and select the correct option.

I	II
a. Kutcha house	1. Made on wheels
b. Pucca house	2. Made of bamboo, mud, straw, leaves, etc.
c. Igloo	3. Made of wood, bricks, cement, steel, etc.
d. Caravan	4. Made of snow

(A) a-2; b-4; c-1; d-3   (B) a-2; b-1; c-4; d-3
(C) a-2; b-3; c-4; d-1   (D) a-1; b-2; c-3; d-4

27. The given diagram shows the weather conditions. Which season has the 'X' weather condition?

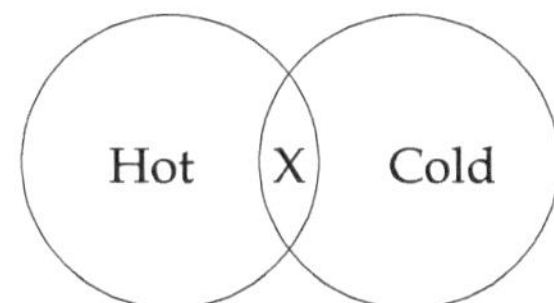

(A) Monsoon   (B) Spring
(C) Summer   (D) Winter

28. Which of the following is not correctly matched?
(A) Igloo - Snow house
(B) Caravan - House on Wheels
(C) Multi Storey - Pucca houses
(D) Houseboat - Mud houses

29. The houses have sloping roof-
(A) To give nice and beautiful look
(B) To protect from heat and dust
(C) To help the rain water slip off easily
(D) None of these

30. Woollen clothes are made up of wool which is obtained from:

(A)    (B) 

(C)    (D) 

FAMILY AND FESTIVALS, OCCUPATIONS

LEARNING OBJECTIVES

➤ Types of families
➤ Our festivals

➤ Family tree
➤ Different occupations

MULTIPLE CHOICE QUESTIONS

Direction: Select the correct option for each of the following questions.

1. Ram and Gauri live with their mother and father in Delhi. What type of family is this?
    (A) Small family
    (B) Big family
    (C) Joint family
    (D) Small or nuclear family

2. Our great grandfathers are called _______.
    (A) Ancestors
    (B) Early man
    (C) Old man
    (D) Hominids

3. Early man is called _______.
    (A) Hominids
    (B) Apes
    (C) Hunters and gatherers
    (D) Stone age man

4. Sharing and caring involves _______.
    (A) Taking care of grandparents
    (B) Sharing a meal with brothers and sisters

    (C) Helping younger brothers and/ sisters in their work
    (D) All of these

5. Which of these is not a family occasion?
    (A) Lakshmi puja   (B) Langar
    (C) Wedding   (D) Birthday

6. Which of these is a part of recreation but our parents suggest that we should avoid it?
    (A) Listening to music
    (B) Watching TV
    (C) Watching cartoons for long time
    (D) Practising yoga

7. Traits are _______.
    (A) Resembling habits
    (B) Resembling physical characteristics
    (C) Resembling genes
    (D) All of these

8. How many generations are included when you use the term **grand** as prefix of father, with respect to you?
    (A) 1   (B) 2
    (C) 3   (D) 4

9. You can resemble in traits with your __________.

(A) Cousin   (B) Uncle

(C) Grandmother   (D) All of these

10. One family tree spreads into __________ families:

(A) 2   (B) 3

(C) 4   (D) Many

11. Match the following __________.

a. Green-grocer   i. bakes bread

b. Chemist   ii. flies an aeroplane

c. Baker   iii. sells medicines

d. Magician   iv. sells vegetables

e. Pilot   v. shows magic

(A) a-iv, b-iii, c-i, d-v, e-ii

(B) a-iv, b-iii, c-i, d-ii, e-v

(C) a-iv, b-i, c-iii, d-v, e-i

(D) a-iii, b-iv, c-i, d-v, e-i

12. Shikha got married to Chander. Chander is Shikha's __________.

(A) Fiancé

(B) Spouse

(C) Husband

(D) Both (B) and (C)

13. Mahatma Gandhi is also called the father of the nation. People go to his *samadhi* at __________, __________ to pay their respects.

(A) Raj Ghat, New Delhi

(B) New Delhi, Raj Ghat

(C) Raj Ghat, Bhopal

(D) Mumbai, Raj Ghat

14. Dr. Sarvepalli Radhakhrishnan's birthday is celebrated as __________.

(A) Children's Day

(B) Father's day

(C) Teacher's Day

(D) None of these

15. Chacha Nehru's birthday is celebrated as __________.

(A) Children's Day

(B) Father's day

(C) Teacher's Day

(D) None of these

16. What is the prayer of Muslims called?

(A) Aarti

(B) Bhajan

(C) Prayer

(D) Namaz

17. On this day Hindus do Lakshmi puja at home __________.

(A) Holi   (B) Onam

(C) Diwali   (D) Gurupurab

18. A Langar is organized on this day, where everyone gets free food. Name the festival.

(A) Diwali   (B) Onam

(C) Lohri   (D) Gurupurab

19. Name the harvest festival of Kerala

(A) Pongal   (B) Onam

(C) Lohri   (D) Holi

20. Name the harvest festival of Tamil Nadu

(A) Pongal   (B) Onam

(C) Lohri   (D) Holi

21. Which of the following festivals is celebrated on the same day every year?

(A) Janmashtmi

(B) Christmas

(C) Rakshabandhan

(D) Diwali

22. Who was the first Guru of the Sikhs?

(A) Guru Arjan Singh

(B) Guru Govind Singh

(C) Guru Nanak

(D) Guru Teg Bahadur

23. Which of the following festivals is celebrated in the spring season?
    (A) Teej
    (B) Dussehra
    (C) Raksha bandhan
    (D) Holi

24. This/these festival(s) is/are celebrated by Christians __________.
    (A) Good Friday
    (B) Eid-ul Fiter
    (C) Easter
    (D) Both (A) and (C)

25. Eid is celebrated by __________.
    (A) Hindus   (B) Muslims
    (C) Christians   (D) Sikhs

26. Name the person who mends our shoes
    (A) Florist   (B) Cobbler
    (C) Grocer   (D) Barber

27. What does a soldier do?
    (A) Cuts and trims our hair.
    (B) Grows food grains.
    (C) Protect the country from enemies.
    (D) Builds houses

28. We take help from __________ when we need flowers to gift someone?
    (A) Postman   (B) Florist
    (C) Mason   (D) Plumber

29. Ananya's tap is not working properly, she should call a __________.
    (A) Postman   (B) Florist
    (C) Mason   (D) Plumber

30. The bed in which you sleep is made by __________.
    (A) Postman   (B) Carpenter
    (C) Mason   (D) Plumber

HOTS (ACHIEVERS SECTION)

31. Match column I with column II and select the correct option.

I	II
A. Children's Day	1. Mahatma Gandhi
B. Teacher's Day	2. Lal Bahadur Shastri
C. Raj Ghat, New Delhi	3. Chacha Nehru
D. 2nd October	4. Dr. Sarvepalli Radhakhrishnan

    (A) A-4; B-3; C-1; D-2
    (B) A-3; B-4; C-1; D-2
    (C) A-4; B-2; C-1; D-3
    (D) A-1; B-3; C-4; D-2

32. Match column I with column II and select the correct option.

I	II
A. Police man	1. Fire station
B. Doctor	2. Police station
C. Postman	3. Hospital
D. Fireman	4. Post office

    (A) A-2; B-3; C-4; D-1
    (B) A-1; B-3; C-4; d-2
    (C) A-2; B-1; C-4; D-3
    (D) A-2; B-3; C-1; D-4

33. Match the following

	List I		List II
A.	Eid	1.	Hindi
B.	Diwali	2.	Sikh
C.	Guruparva	3.	Christian
D.	Christmas	4.	Muslim

(A) A-1, B-2, C-4, D-1
(B) A-2, B-3, C-1, D-2
(C) A-3, B-4, C-3, D-4
(D) A-4, B-1, C-2, D-3

34. Which of the following statements is wrong?
    (A) Relaxation helps us to feel rested and happy.
    (B) Stamp collection is an outdoor activity.
    (C) Drawing is an indoor activity.
    (D) Swimming is an outdoor activity.

35. Consider the two statements and choose the correct option.

    Statement 1: The main function of Gandhi Jayanti is held at the Raj ghat.

    Statement 2: Guruparvas is celebrated on the birthday of 10 Sikh Gurus.
    (A) Statement is true, statement 2 is false.
    (B) Statement 1 is false, statement 2 is true.
    (C) Both the statements are true.
    (D) Both the statements are false.

1.	Ⓐ	Ⓑ	Ⓒ	Ⓓ	8.	Ⓐ	Ⓑ	Ⓒ	Ⓓ	15.	Ⓐ	Ⓑ	Ⓒ	Ⓓ	22	Ⓐ	Ⓑ	Ⓒ	Ⓓ	29.	Ⓐ	Ⓑ	Ⓒ	Ⓓ
2.	Ⓐ	Ⓑ	Ⓒ	Ⓓ	9.	Ⓐ	Ⓑ	Ⓒ	Ⓓ	16.	Ⓐ	Ⓑ	Ⓒ	Ⓓ	23.	Ⓐ	Ⓑ	Ⓒ	Ⓓ	30.	Ⓐ	Ⓑ	Ⓒ	Ⓓ
3.	Ⓐ	Ⓑ	Ⓒ	Ⓓ	10.	Ⓐ	Ⓑ	Ⓒ	Ⓓ	17.	Ⓐ	Ⓑ	Ⓒ	Ⓓ	24.	Ⓐ	Ⓑ	Ⓒ	Ⓓ	31.	Ⓐ	Ⓑ	Ⓒ	Ⓓ
4.	Ⓐ	Ⓑ	Ⓒ	Ⓓ	11.	Ⓐ	Ⓑ	Ⓒ	Ⓓ	18.	Ⓐ	Ⓑ	Ⓒ	Ⓓ	25.	Ⓐ	Ⓑ	Ⓒ	Ⓓ	32.	Ⓐ	Ⓑ	Ⓒ	Ⓓ
5.	Ⓐ	Ⓑ	Ⓒ	Ⓓ	12.	Ⓐ	Ⓑ	Ⓒ	Ⓓ	19.	Ⓐ	Ⓑ	Ⓒ	Ⓓ	26.	Ⓐ	Ⓑ	Ⓒ	Ⓓ	33.	Ⓐ	Ⓑ	Ⓒ	Ⓓ
6.	Ⓐ	Ⓑ	Ⓒ	Ⓓ	13.	Ⓐ	Ⓑ	Ⓒ	Ⓓ	20.	Ⓐ	Ⓑ	Ⓒ	Ⓓ	27.	Ⓐ	Ⓑ	Ⓒ	Ⓓ	34.	Ⓐ	Ⓑ	Ⓒ	Ⓓ
7.	Ⓐ	Ⓑ	Ⓒ	Ⓓ	14.	Ⓐ	Ⓑ	Ⓒ	Ⓓ	21.	Ⓐ	Ⓑ	Ⓒ	Ⓓ	28.	Ⓐ	Ⓑ	Ⓒ	Ⓓ	35.	Ⓐ	Ⓑ	Ⓒ	Ⓓ

GOOD HABITS AND SAFETY RULES

LEARNING OBJECTIVES

➤ Good habits
➤ Safety rules

MULTIPLE CHOICE QUESTIONS

1. Which of the following activities we should do every morning?
   (A) Cooking
   (B) Bathing
   (C) Brushing
   (D) Both (B) and (C)

2. Which of the following is a good habit?
   (A) Bite your nails daily
   (B) Take bath daily
   (C) Dance on the road
   (D) Wash your hand before going to toilet

3. It is not a good habit to _____.
   (A) throw waste in the dustbin,
   (B) put clean water for birds to drink.
   (C) waste food by taking excels food.
   (D) eat healthy food.

4. _________ is the immediate help given to a person who is hurt, before the doctor comes.
   (A) Critical aid
   (B) First aid
   (C) Medical treatment
   (D) Intensive treatment

5. Green light means _____.
   (A) come
   (B) run
   (C) go
   (D) dance

6. Which of the following we use while crossing the road?
   (A) Footpath
   (B) Zebra crossing
   (C) Traffic light
   (D) Both (B) and (C)

7. It is NOT necessary to wash your hands _____.
   (A) before eating
   (B) after eating
   (C) both (A) & (B)
   (D) after bathing

8. At home, never play with _________.
   (A) teddy bear
   (B) knife
   (C) ball
   (D) video game

9. Which of the following activity we should do with the help of an adult?

OLYMPIAD WORKBOOK (NSO) CLASS−2

(A) Eating food
(B) Playing with teddy bear
(C) Learning swimming
(D) Bathing

10. Which of the following activities you should never do in the playground?
    (A) Jump off a see-saw
    (B) Go slow on slides
    (C) Wait for your turn on slides
    (D) None of these

11. At homes, stay away from__________.
    (A) toys
    (B) knife
    (C) match box
    (D) Both (B) and (C)

12. Which of the following is a good habit?
    (A) Washing hand before going to toilet.
    (B) Washing hand before and after eating food.
    (C) Brushing teeth once in week.
    (D) All of the above.

13. Which of the following is correct option for traffic signal?
    (A) Red > stop
    (B) Blue > go
    (c) Green> go
    (D) Both (A) and (B)

14. Which of the following item should be used if a person gets minor cut?
    (A) Cold cream
    (B) Ice pack
    (C) Antiseptic lotion
    (D) None of these

15. Which of the following articles of your home should not be touched with wet hands?
    (A) Toys
    (B) Knife

(C) Gas stove
(D) Electric switch

16. Which of the following activities keeps your bones and muscles strong?
    (A) Brushing
    (B) Bathing
    (C) Exercise
    (D) Eating

17. Which of the following rules we should follow when we are in swimming pool?
    (A) Jump into the swimming pool
    (B) Do not go deep inside the swimming pool
    (C) Do not enter alone in the swimming pool
    (D) Both (B) and (C)

18. What we shouldn't do while walking on road?
    (A) Walking on footpath.
    (B) Running to cross the road.
    (C) Using zebra crossing to cross the road.
    (D) All the above

19. Which one of the following we should follow while in/on a school bus?
    (A) Leaning out of the window of the bus.
    (B) Get down from the moving bus.
    (C) Stand in queue to get into the bus.
    (D) Running in a moving bus.

20. Which of the following is not a rule for play ground?
    (A) We should play by turn.
    (B) We shouldn't climb the broken swing.
    (C) We should make the playground dirty.
    (D) We should not fight when we lose.

21. Match the given columns and select the correct option.

Safety rules	Activity
(a) Keep sitting	(1) Playing
(b) Take a rubber tube	(2) Swimming
(c) Use a park or garden	(3) Travelling
(d) Use the footpath	(4) Walking

(A) (a)-(1), (b)-(2), (c)-(4), (d)-(3)
(B) (a)-(3), (b)-(2), (c)-(1), (d)-(4)
(C) (a)-(3), (b)-(2), (c)-(4), (d)-(1)
(D) (a)-(2), (b)-(3), (c)-(1), (d)-(4)

22. Refer to the safety rules written on the board.

When you swim
1. Do not play rough games in the pool.
2. Always swim in the deep end.
3. Always take a rubber tube with you.
4. Avoid swimming with a grown-up near you.

Which of the safety rules is/are INCORRECT?
(A) 1 and 3 only   (B) 4 only
(C) 2 and 4 only   (D) 1, 2 and 3 only

23. Ramesh takes healthy diet daily still he falls ill frequently. What could be the reason for it?
(A) He does not comb his hair daily. done clear
(B) He does not trim his nails regularly. done clear
(C) He does not wash his hands properly before eating. done clear
(D) Both (B) and (C)

24. The given things can be dangerous as they all

(A) Have sharp edges which can cut your hands
(B) Can catch fire easily and can burn you
(C) Are chemicals and can be harmful
(D) None of these.

25. Ashok goes to school on a bicycle. Which of these safety rules should he follow?
(A) He should keep to the right of the road.
(B) He should give signals before taking turns.
(C) He should cross the road by using zebra crossing.
(D) All of these

Darken Your Choice with HB Pencil

1.	Ⓐ Ⓑ Ⓒ Ⓓ	6.	Ⓐ Ⓑ Ⓒ Ⓓ	11.	Ⓐ Ⓑ Ⓒ Ⓓ	16	Ⓐ Ⓑ Ⓒ Ⓓ	21.	Ⓐ Ⓑ Ⓒ Ⓓ
2.	Ⓐ Ⓑ Ⓒ Ⓓ	7.	Ⓐ Ⓑ Ⓒ Ⓓ	12.	Ⓐ Ⓑ Ⓒ Ⓓ	17.	Ⓐ Ⓑ Ⓒ Ⓓ	22.	Ⓐ Ⓑ Ⓒ Ⓓ
3.	Ⓐ Ⓑ Ⓒ Ⓓ	8.	Ⓐ Ⓑ Ⓒ Ⓓ	13.	Ⓐ Ⓑ Ⓒ Ⓓ	18.	Ⓐ Ⓑ Ⓒ Ⓓ	23.	Ⓐ Ⓑ Ⓒ Ⓓ
4.	Ⓐ Ⓑ Ⓒ Ⓓ	9.	Ⓐ Ⓑ Ⓒ Ⓓ	14.	Ⓐ Ⓑ Ⓒ Ⓓ	19.	Ⓐ Ⓑ Ⓒ Ⓓ	24.	Ⓐ Ⓑ Ⓒ Ⓓ
5.	Ⓐ Ⓑ Ⓒ Ⓓ	10.	Ⓐ Ⓑ Ⓒ Ⓓ	15.	Ⓐ Ⓑ Ⓒ Ⓓ	20.	Ⓐ Ⓑ Ⓒ Ⓓ	25.	Ⓐ Ⓑ Ⓒ Ⓓ

TRANSPORT AND COMMUNICATION

- ➤ Public and private transport
- ➤ Early modes of communication
- ➤ Advanced modes of communication

MULTIPLE CHOICE QUESTIONS

Direction: Select the correct option for each of the following questions.

1. Animal carts like bullock cart, horse cart (tonga), cycles, and large sea ships are examples of __________.
   (A) Fast transport
   (B) Slow transport
   (C) Public transport
   (D) Private transport

2. Which of these can further be divided into categories like public and private transport?
   (A) Modes of transport
   (B) Means of communication
   (C) Slow transport
   (D) Fast transport

3. Bicycle, motor bike, and car are examples of __________.
   (A) Public transport
   (B) Private transport
   (C) Fast transport
   (D) Slow transport

4. Pigeons are an example of __________.
   (A) Modern mode of communication
   (B) Early mode of communication
   (C) Slow mode of communication
   (D) Both (B) and (C)

5. Which of the following improved the way of communication?
   (A) Invention of telephone
   (B) Invention of television
   (C) Invention of radio
   (D) All of these

6. Latest modes of communication is/are __________.
   (A) Telephone   (B) Telegram
   (C) Mobile   (D) Both (A) and (C)

7. We should cross the road only when the traffic light is __________.
   (A) Blue for the traffic
   (B) Red for the traffic
   (C) Yellow for the traffic
   (D) Green for the traffic

8. When you cross the road __________.
   (A) Look to the left, then to the right, and again to the right before crossing
   (B) Look to the left and then to the right before crossing
   (C) Look to the right, then to the left, and again to the right before crossing
   (D) Look to the right and cross the road

9. Which of the following is the cheapest means of transport?

(A)  (B) 

(C)  (D) 

10. Which of the following modes of transportation can be run by a gas engine?

(A)  (B) 

(C)  (D) Both (A) and (B)

11. Which of the following modes of transport is run by manpower?
(A) Bicycle (B) Bus
(C) Ship (D) Auto rickshaw

12. PIN stands for __________.
(A) Postal Index Number
(B) Personal Identification Number
(C) Personal Index Number
(D) Postal Identification Number

13. Distance is measured in __________.
(A) Km
(B) Meter
(C) Kg
(D) Both (A) and (B)

14. When a traffic police officer signals to stop vehicles, he must approach from the __________.
(A) Front side
(B) Behind
(C) Left and right sides
(D) Both (A) and (B)

15. Which among the following is likely to be involved in a two-way communication?
(A) Radio jockey (B) Editor
(C) Businessman (D) Manager

16. Which is the best example of "means of mass communication"?
(A) Television (B) Letter
(C) Telephone (D) Telegram

17. The below picture signifies __________.

(A) Fastest means of communication
(B) E-mail
(C) Slowest means of communication
(D) Both (A) and (B)

18. This means of communication carries a message more quickly than a telegram.
(A) Fax
(B) Letter
(C) Pigeon
(D) None of these

19. Which means of communication was used in the past to send messages faster than letters?
(A) Pigeon
(B) Telegram
(C) Radio
(D) Fax

20. Which of the following is an example of auto-visual means of communication?
(A) Radio
(B) Television
(C) Tape recorder
(D) Speaker

21. Which of the following is the fastest means of two-way communication?
(A) Loudspeaker
(B) Emails
(C) Telephone
(D) Letter

OLYMPIAD WORKBOOK (NSO) CLASS—2

22. The below symbol signifies __________.

   (A) Smoking is prohibited here
   (B) Hospital is straight ahead and near the given place
   (C) Parking is prohibited here
   (D) None of these

23. The below symbols signifies __________.

24. The below icon is for __________.

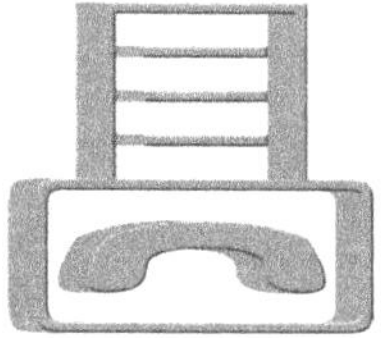

   (A) A telephone
   (B) A fax machine
   (C) A telephone booth
   (D) An e-mail

25. Which type of phone, we can carry in pocket?
   (A) Mobile phone   (B) Desktop
   (C) laptop   (D) All of these

(A) Red light
(B) Pedestrian crossing
(C) Zebra crossing
(D) Both (B) and (C)

HOTS (ACHIEVERS SECTION)

26. Find the odd one out.
   (A) E-mail; Twitter; Facebook; You tube
   (B) Twitter; Facebook; LinkedIn; You tube
   (C) Facebook; LinkedIn; You tube; Twitter
   (D) LinkedIn; Facebook; Twitter; You tube

27. Match column I with column II and select the correct option.

I	II
A. Metro train	1. Runs on diesel
B. Bicycle	2. Runs on electricity
C. Truck	3. Runs by animal
D. Bullock cart	4. Runs by manpower

   (A) A-3; B-2; C-4; D-1
   (B) A-2; B-4; C-3; D-1
   (C) A-4; B-2; C-1; D-3
   (D) A-2; B-4; C-1; D-3

28. Select the INCORRECT match
   (A) Urgent messages - Letters
   (B) Telephone   - STD, ISD
   (C) Internet   - E-mail
   (D) Picture news   - TV

29. A __________ carries a message more quickly than a __________. You can talk to the person directly.
   (A) Fax, Telegram
   (A) Fax, telephone
   (C) Telephone, Telegram
   (D) Email, Fax

30. Consider the following statement and choose the correct option.

Statement A: Water transport is the fastest means of transport.

Statement B: Newspaper, Radio and Television are the means of mass communication.

(A) Statement 'A' is true, statement 'B' is false.

(B) Statement 'B' is true, statement 'A' is false.

(C) Both the statements are true.

(D) Both the statements are false.

1. (A) (B) (C) (D)	7. (A) (B) (C) (D)	13. (A) (B) (C) (D)	19 (A) (B) (C) (D)	25. (A) (B) (C) (D)
2. (A) (B) (C) (D)	8. (A) (B) (C) (D)	14. (A) (B) (C) (D)	20. (A) (B) (C) (D)	26. (A) (B) (C) (D)
3. (A) (B) (C) (D)	9. (A) (B) (C) (D)	15. (A) (B) (C) (D)	21. (A) (B) (C) (D)	27. (A) (B) (C) (D)
4. (A) (B) (C) (D)	10. (A) (B) (C) (D)	16. (A) (B) (C) (D)	22. (A) (B) (C) (D)	28. (A) (B) (C) (D)
5. (A) (B) (C) (D)	11. (A) (B) (C) (D)	17. (A) (B) (C) (D)	23. (A) (B) (C) (D)	29. (A) (B) (C) (D)
6. (A) (B) (C) (D)	12. (A) (B) (C) (D)	18. (A) (B) (C) (D)	24. (A) (B) (C) (D)	30. (A) (B) (C) (D)

OLYMPIAD WORKBOOK (NSO) CLASS – 2

AIR, WATER AND ROCKS 

- ➤ Air
- ➤ Water
- ➤ Rocks

MULTIPLE CHOICE QUESTIONS

Direction: Select the correct option for each of the following questions.

1. Air is made up of __________.
   (A) Liquids (B) Solids
   (C) Gases (D) All of these
2. Which of these helps us to fly a kite?
   (A) Wind (B) Breeze
   (C) Air (D) All of these
3. Which of these make the air clean?
   (A) Human beings
   (B) Green plants
   (C) Animals
   (D) Factories
4. When the air is strong and fast, it is called __________.
   (A) Storm (B) Breeze
   (C) Wind (D) Air
5. The air that we breathe in should be __________.
   (A) Fresh
   (B) Warm and dirty
   (C) Fresh and cold
   (D) Cold and dirty
6. When water is heated, it changes into __________.
   (A) Rain
   (B) Water vapour
   (C) Ice
   (D) Smoke
7. We feel __________ on our face when we run very fast.
   (A) Water vapour
   (B) Dust
   (C) Air
   (D) Smoke
8. Which is the purest form of water?
   (A) River water (B) Sea water
   (C) Rain water (D) Pond water
9. Boiling of water is good because it __________.
   (A) Purifies the water
   (B) Kills the germs
   (C) Makes water drinkable
   (D) Kills the germs, purifies it, and makes it drinkable
10. Rain water goes __________.
    (A) Below the trees roots
    (B) Below the soil
    (C) Below the ponds
    (D) In the sky again

11. Which statement is completely correct?
    (A) Washing clothes in the river and not supplying waste material from factories into the rivers.
    (B) Taking domestic animals to the rivers to give them a bath and not throwing domestic garbage into the rivers.
    (C) Using home pits to burn domestic garbage.
    (D) Washing clothes in the rivers and throwing waste from factories into the rivers.

12. Which of these has been put under the wrong heading?

Solid	Liquid	Gas
Molten candle	Lime juice	Water vapour
Eraser	Molten ice	Gas inside the air conditioner

    (A) Molten ice
    (B) Molten candle
    (C) Water vapour
    (D) Eraser

13. The layer of air which surrounds the Earth is called the __________.
    (A) Atmosphere
    (B) Rainfall
    (C) Weather
    (D) Temperature

14. Clouds are made up of __________.
    (A) Water vapour
    (B) Steam
    (C) Tiny water droplets
    (D) Air

15. Air occupies space and has __________.
    (A) Force
    (B) Temperature
    (C) Weight
    (D) Both (A) and (B)

16. Water can exist in how many states?
    (A) 2   (B) 4
    (C) 5   (D) 3

17. In which form of water can we not see it?
    (A) Solid   (B) Gas
    (C) Liquid   (D) Steam

18. Windmills are used to __________.
    (A) Grind grains
    (B) Pump water
    (C) Produce electricity
    (D) All of these

19. What is evaporation?
    (A) It is the changing of water into water vapour by heating
    (B) It is the changing of water into ice by cooling
    (C) It is the changing of ice into water by heating
    (D) It is the changing of ice into water vapour by heating

20. Look at the picture given below. It represents __________.

    (A) Air pollution
    (B) Air waves
    (C) Storm
    (D) Heavy rain with strong wind

21. Fast and strong winds are called __________.
    (A) Earthquakes   (B) Storm
    (C) Wind   (D) Breeze

22. When sunlight passes through water droplets, a ______ is formed in the sky.
    (A) Cloud   (B) Pattern
    (C) Rainbow   (D) Star

23. Which of these activities does not need wind?

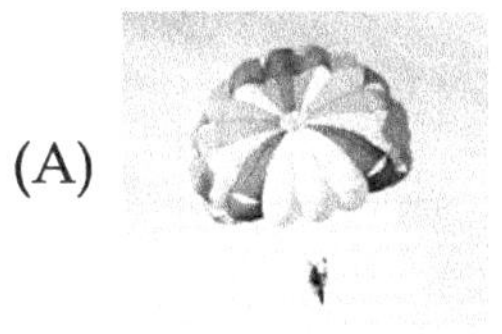 (A)  (B)

 (C)  (D)

24. Which of these do we need to stay alive?
    (A) Soil
    (B) Water
    (C) Air
    (D) Both (B) and (C)

25. When water vapour cools down, it is called:
    (A) Melting   (B) Freezing
    (C) Condensation   (D) Evaporation

26. Which of these are built to use surface water?
    (A) Canals   (B) Wells
    (C) Dams   (D) Both (A) and (C)

27. Which of these pushes the water in the ocean and causes waves?
    (A) Fishes
    (B) Wind
    (C) Rocks
    (D) Both (A) and (B)

28. Which of the following is not a source of surface water?
    (A) Puddle   (B) Well
    (C) Pond   (D) River

29. Boiling water is not completely pure water because it cannot:
    (A) Kill the germs
    (B) Filter the salt present in water
    (C) Filter the particles present in water
    (D) Both (B) and (C)

30. Look at the picture given below.

The lead in pencil is made of _______.
    (A) Graphite   (B) Granite
    (C) Sandstone   (D) Coal

HOTS (ACHIEVERS SECTION)

31. The following picture shows a balance. One side of the balance holds an empty balloon. The other side holds the same kind of balloon full of air. Which property of air is shown by the balance?

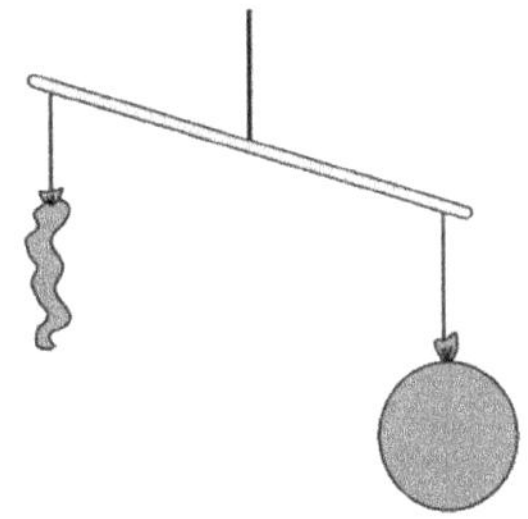

    (A) Air is solid
    (B) Air has heat
    (C) Air has weight
    (D) Air is energy

32. When a cup of water at room temperature is put in a freezer, the water's state of matter will change from:
    (A) Liquid to gas
    (B) Gas to liquid
    (C) Liquid to solid
    (D) Solid to liquid

33. Look at the figure given below and identify the given rock.

(A) Graphite   (B) Limestone
(C) Diamond   (D) Gemstone

34. Match the following rocks in Column-I with their uses in Column-II.

	Column-I		Column-II
p.	Gemstones	i.	Pots
q.	Slate	ii.	Roofs
r.	Granite	iii.	Jewellery
s.	China clay	iv.	Floors

(A) p-iii, q-ii, r-iv, s-i
(B) p-ii, q-iii, r-i, s-iv
(C) p-i, q-iv, r-ii, s-iii
(D) p-iii, q-i, r-iv, s-ii

35. ___________ is the softest mineral and ___________ is the hardest mineral.

(A) Granite, sandstone
(B) Talc, diamond
(C) Diamond, granite
(D) Sandstone, granite

EARTH AND UNIVERSE

10

LEARNING OBJECTIVES

- ➤ Earth and its structure
- ➤ Earth's rotation – day and night
- ➤ The Moon
- ➤ The Sun
- ➤ Light and shadow

MULTIPLE CHOICE QUESTIONS

Direction: Select the correct option for each of the following questions.

1. The Earth rotates _________.
   - (A) On its axis
   - (B) Around the Sun
   - (C) Around the Moon
   - (D) Around the planets

2. The Sun helps the Earth by _________.
   - (A) Giving it heat and light
   - (B) Making plants grow on it
   - (C) Providing it with food and water
   - (D) All of these

3. The shape of a shadow changes according to _________.
   - (A) The movement of the Moon
   - (B) The size of the object
   - (C) The movement of the Sun
   - (D) All of these

4. The Earth rotates in a _________ path.
   - (A) Straight
   - (B) Anti-clockwise
   - (C) Clockwise
   - (D) Zigzag

5. _________ Moon is three-fourth lit up.
   - (A) Crescent
   - (B) Gibbous
   - (C) Quarter
   - (D) Full

6. When there is no Moon, it is called _________.
   - (A) New Moon
   - (B) Full Moon
   - (C) Crescent Moon
   - (D) Half Moon

7. Which of the following is not a shape of the Moon?
   - (A) Crescent
   - (B) Full Moon
   - (C) New Moon
   - (D) Waning

8. Where is a shadow formed?
   - (A) Near the source of light
   - (B) Opposite to the source of light
   - (C) Both (A) and (B)
   - (D) None of these

9. Radium light is a _________.
   - (A) Source of light and indicator
   - (B) An indicator
   - (C) A decorator
   - (D) Symbol of light

10. Which of the following is not a source of light?
    - (A) The Sun
    - (B) The Moon
    - (C) Star
    - (D) Rainbow

11. Which of these is a star?
    - (A) The Moon
    - (B) The Sun
    - (C) The Earth
    - (D) The Venus

12. How much time does the Earth take to complete one rotation?
   (A) 24 hours   (B) One day
   (C) 365 hours   (D) Both (A) and (B)

13. A globe is a model of ________.
   (A) The Sun   (B) The Planet
   (C) The Earth   (D) Star

14. Which is the smallest planet in the solar system?
   (A) Venus   (B) Mercury
   (C) Earth   (D) Neptune

15. In the picture below, the planet is revolving around the Sun on its ______.

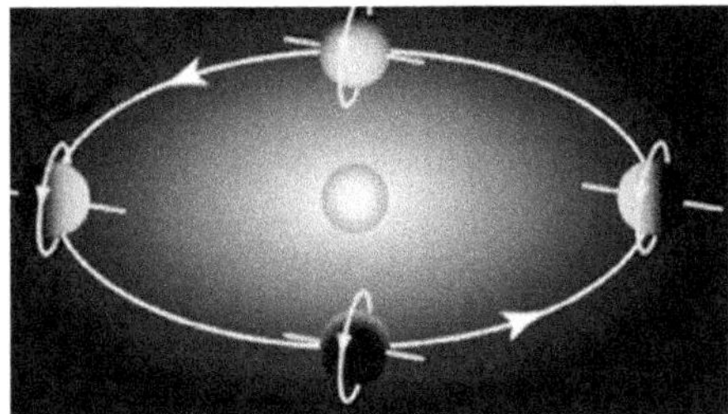

   (A) Track   (B) Orbit
   (C) Axis   (D) None of these

16. What are the major land masses of the Earth called?
   (A) Islands   (B) Continents
   (C) Plateaus   (D) Mountains

17. They are the major water masses on the Earth. They are called ________.
   (A) Islands   (B) Continents
   (C) Oceans   (D) Rivers

18. An area of fairly level high ground is called ________.
   (A) Mountain   (B) Plain
   (C) Plateau   (D) Continent

19. Which of these represents the surface of the Earth?
   (A) Plateau   (B) Plain
   (C) Landform   (D) All of these

20. When we land on the Moon, we ________.
   (A) Can see earth from there because moon gives its own light
   (B) Can see earth from there because earth reflects sunlight
   (C) Cannot see earth from there because moon reflects sunlight
   (D) Cannot see Earth from there because Earth gives its own light

21. Which of these is the correct statement?
   (A) The full moon day is called Amavasya
   (B) A new moon day is called Purnima
   (C) Moon has light of its own
   (D) The Sun is a star

22. Which of these is also called a full-moon day?
   (A) Crescent moon
   (B) New moon day
   (C) Purnima
   (D) Amavasya

23. How much area of the Earth is covered by water?
   (A) About 1/4th   (B) About 2/3rd
   (C) About 3/4th   (D) About 1/2

24. Identify the figure below. Its shape is ________.
   (A) Globe, spherical
   (B) Globe, round
   (C) Globe, flat
   (D) Earth, spherical

25. A full moon has no ________.
   (A) Shadow on it
   (B) Light on it
   (C) Shape on it
   (D) Phase on it

26. Which thing near this house will wash away the MOST during heavy rain?

(A) Gravel driveway
(B) Dirt pile
(C) Stepping stones
(D) Soil under grass

27. Refer the given diagram of the solar system.

  I.   Which of them denotes the correct position of the moon?

  II. Who was the first person to step on the moon?

	I	II
(A)	Q	Neil Armstrong
(B)	P	Neil Armstrong
(C)	R	Alyssa Carson
(D)	S	Kalpana Chawla

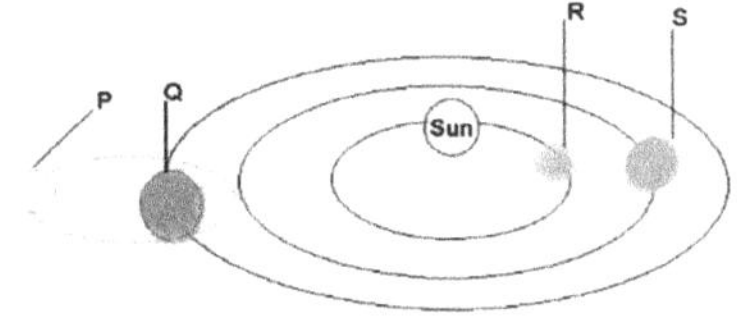

28. Select the correct option from the following.
(A) Unlike Moon, stars give their own light.
(B) Unlike stars, Moon gives its own light.
(C) Like Moon, stars shine by reflecting Sun's light.
(D) Like stars, Moon appears twinkling in the night sky.

29. Observe the given figure. What is the time of the day?

(A) Morning   (B) Noon
(C) Afternoon   (D) Evening

30. The day and night are caused due to __________ of Earth on its ______.
(A) Revolution, Axis
(B) Rotation, Axis
(C) Revolution, Orbit
(D) Rotation, Orbit

Darken Your Choice with HB Pencil

1.	Ⓐ Ⓑ Ⓒ Ⓓ	7.	Ⓐ Ⓑ Ⓒ Ⓓ	13.	Ⓐ Ⓑ Ⓒ Ⓓ	19	Ⓐ Ⓑ Ⓒ Ⓓ	25.	Ⓐ Ⓑ Ⓒ Ⓓ
2.	Ⓐ Ⓑ Ⓒ Ⓓ	8.	Ⓐ Ⓑ Ⓒ Ⓓ	14.	Ⓐ Ⓑ Ⓒ Ⓓ	20.	Ⓐ Ⓑ Ⓒ Ⓓ	26.	Ⓐ Ⓑ Ⓒ Ⓓ
3.	Ⓐ Ⓑ Ⓒ Ⓓ	9.	Ⓐ Ⓑ Ⓒ Ⓓ	15.	Ⓐ Ⓑ Ⓒ Ⓓ	21.	Ⓐ Ⓑ Ⓒ Ⓓ	27.	Ⓐ Ⓑ Ⓒ Ⓓ
4.	Ⓐ Ⓑ Ⓒ Ⓓ	10.	Ⓐ Ⓑ Ⓒ Ⓓ	16.	Ⓐ Ⓑ Ⓒ Ⓓ	22.	Ⓐ Ⓑ Ⓒ Ⓓ	28.	Ⓐ Ⓑ Ⓒ Ⓓ
5.	Ⓐ Ⓑ Ⓒ Ⓓ	11.	Ⓐ Ⓑ Ⓒ Ⓓ	17.	Ⓐ Ⓑ Ⓒ Ⓓ	23.	Ⓐ Ⓑ Ⓒ Ⓓ	29.	Ⓐ Ⓑ Ⓒ Ⓓ
6.	Ⓐ Ⓑ Ⓒ Ⓓ	12.	Ⓐ Ⓑ Ⓒ Ⓓ	18.	Ⓐ Ⓑ Ⓒ Ⓓ	24.	Ⓐ Ⓑ Ⓒ Ⓓ	30.	Ⓐ Ⓑ Ⓒ Ⓓ

LOGICAL REASONING 

LEARNING OBJECTIVES

- Finding the relation
- Classification (Odd One Out)
- Letter to letter coding
- Finding the next shape in a series
- Length
- Geometrical lines
- Solving series completion
- Identify the odd object from a group
- Position or rank of an object or a person
- Pictographs
- Mass
- Plane geometrical shapes

MULTIPLE CHOICE QUESTIONS

Direction: Read the options carefully and select the correct alternative.

1. Find out the relation.

   Pen : Ink :: Pencil : ?
   (A) Iron　　　　　　(B) Plastic
   (C) Graphite　　　　(D) Carbon

2. Find out the relation.

   Uttarakhand : Dehradun :: Goa : ?
   (A) Patna　　　　　(B) Panaji
   (C) Jaipur　　　　　(D) Gandhinagar

3. Find the missing shape by identifying the relationship.

   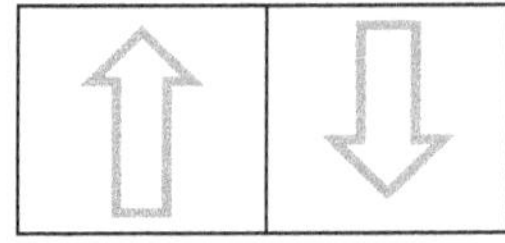 :: 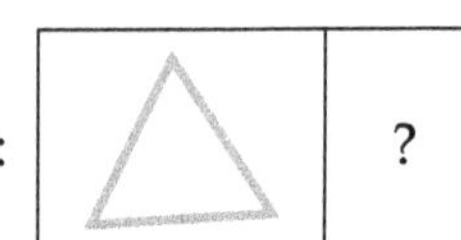

   (A) 　　　　(B) 

   (C) 　　　　(D) 

4. Find the missing shape by identifying the relationship.

   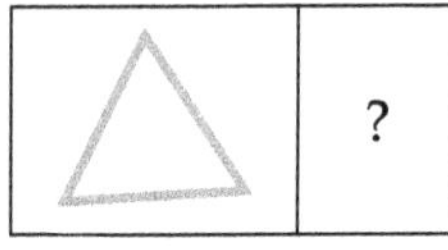

   (A)　　　　　　　　(B)

   (C)　　　　　　　　(D)

5. Find out the relation.

   Father : Mother :: Grandfather : ?
   (A) Grandson
   (B) Daughter
   (C) Grandmother
   (D) Granddaughter

Direction (6–10): Find the next letter in the series given below.

6. C   D   E   F   G   ?
   (A) K   (B) J
   (C) I   (D) H

7. A   D   G   J   M   ?
   (A) O   (B) P
   (C) Q   (D) R

8. D   F   H   J   L   ?
   (A) O   (B) N
   (C) M   (D) P

9. F   G   H   I   J   ?
   (A) N   (B) L
   (C) K   (D) M

10. C   E   G   I   K   ?
   (A) M   (B) N
   (C) O   (D) L

Directions (11–15): In each of the following questions choose the one which is different from the others.

11. (A) Cow   (B) Fish
    (C) Goat   (D) Cat

12. (A) Gold   (B) Iron
    (C) Diamond   (D) Silver

13. (A) Ears   (B) Hands
    (C) Fingers   (D) Eyes

14. (A) Sun   (B) Moon
    (C) Venus   (D) Earth

15. (A) Walk   (B) Run

Direction: Select the correct option for each of the following questions.

16. Choose the odd one out.

    (A)   (B)

    (C)   (D)

17. Choose the odd one out.

    16, 20, 24, 28, 32, 38, 40

    (A) 20   (B) 28
    (C) 32   (D) 38

18. Choose the odd one out.
    (A) Square   (B) Rhombus
    (C) Cube   (D) Rectangle

19. Choose the odd one out.

    (A)   (B)

    (C)   (D)

20. Choose the odd one out.

    (A)   (B)

    (C)   (D)

21. If TABLE is written as 40, then CHAIR will be written as __________
    (A) 39   (B) 38
    (C) 26   (D) 36

22. If CARROT = 75, then RADDISH will be written as __________
    (A) 76   (B) 36
    (C) 63   (D) 85

23. If SEA = 13, then YAK will be written as __________
    (A) 16   (B) 13
    (C) 17   (D) 8

24. If HELP is coded as 8-5-12-16, then how will you code HORSE?
    (A) 8-18-19-15-5   (B) 8-15-5-19-18
    (C) 8-15-18-19-5   (D) 8-19-15-5-18

25. If GOAT is coded as 7-15-1-20, then how will you code SHEEP?
    (A) 19-13-5-5-16
    (B) 19-8-5-13-16
    (C) 19-15-5-5-8
    (D) 19-8-5-5-16

Direction (26–30): Observe the given figures carefully and choose the correct option.

Left (first)

26. Which bird is seventh from the right end?
    (A) M (B) L
    (C) N (D) P

27. Bird O is second to the right of bird ________.
    (A) P (B) I
    (C) M (D) N

28. If bird P and I interchange their positions, then bird ________ is at the left end.
    (A) I (B) L
    (C) P (D) M

29. Bird J is just left to ________ bird.
    (A) N (B) O
    (C) M (D) L

30. Bird ________ is the sixth bird to the right of bird N.
    (A) J (B) K
    (C) M (D) L

31. What are the next two shapes to complete the pattern?

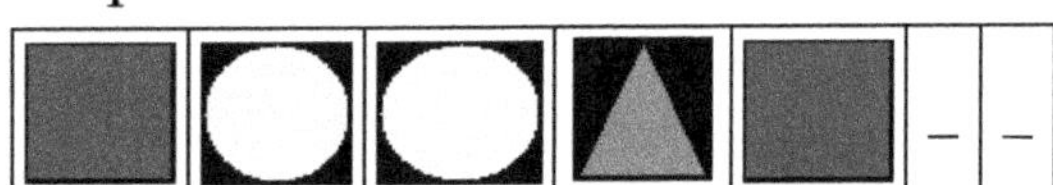

    (A) Circle, circle
    (B) Triangle, circle
    (C) Circle, triangle
    (D) Square, circle

32. What are the next two shapes to complete the pattern?

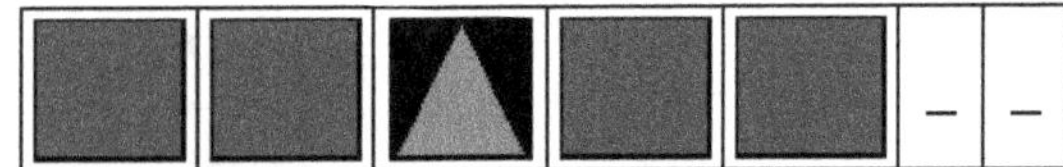

    (A) Circle, circle
    (B) Triangle, square
    (C) Circle, triangle
    (D) Square, circle

33. Find the number pattern in star A. The first point has a value of 3. Then look at star B. Use the same number pattern to figure out the value of the other points.

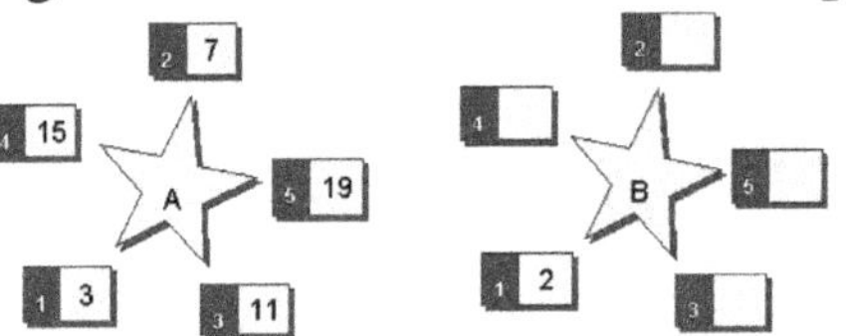

    (A) 5, 7, 9, 18 (B) 4, 6, 8, 10
    (C) 6, 10, 14, 18 (D) 10, 12, 14, 16

34. What number should be on the other points of star B if you follow the same pattern?

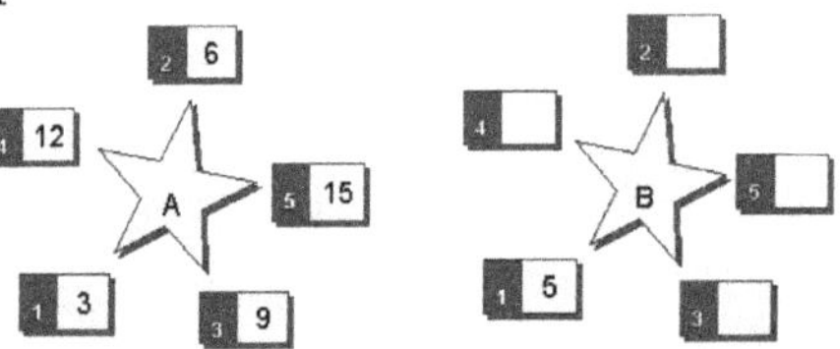

    (A) 5, 7, 9, 18 (B) 10, 11, 15, 17
    (C) 6, 10, 15, 20 (D) 10, 15, 20, 25

35. Write the next 3 numbers in the pattern.
    30, 32, 34, __, __, __
    (A) 36, 38, 40 (B) 34, 36, 38
    (C) 36, 40, 44 (D) None of these

36. Golu won twice as many tokens as Shraddha.
    He could get the ________.
    (A) Robot (B) Teddy bear
    (C) Toy gun (D) Mini computer

37. Jasmine had just enough tokens to exchange for a teddy bear. If she wanted to exchange her tokens for a 2 toy aeroplanes, she will need ________ more tokens.
    (A) 8 (B) 6
    (C) 4 (D) 2

38. Krishna won 30 tokens. He exchanged all of them for two toys. He chose the __________ and the __________.
    (A) Toy gun, toy plane
    (B) Robot, teddy bear
    (C) Robot, mini computer
    (D) Teddy bear, mini computer

Directions (39): Look at the picture graph and answer the question.

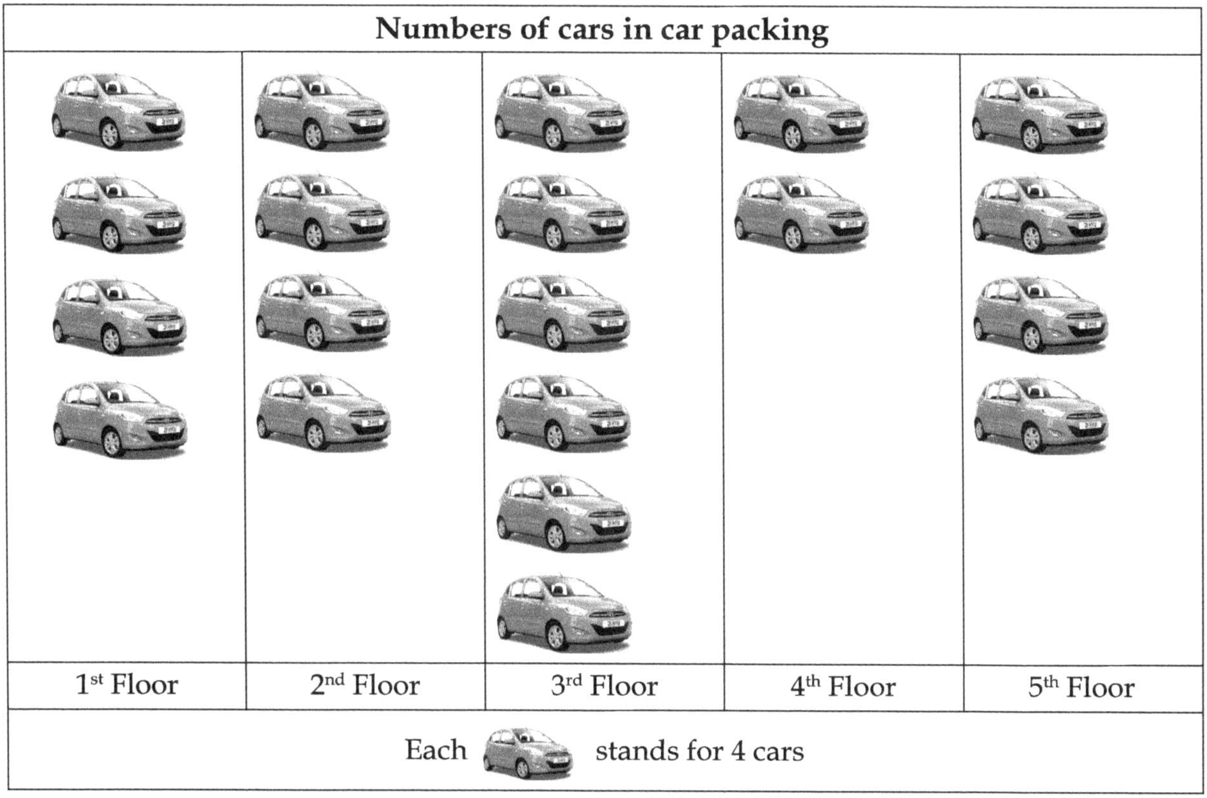

Numbers of cars in car packing				
1st Floor	2nd Floor	3rd Floor	4th Floor	5th Floor

Each 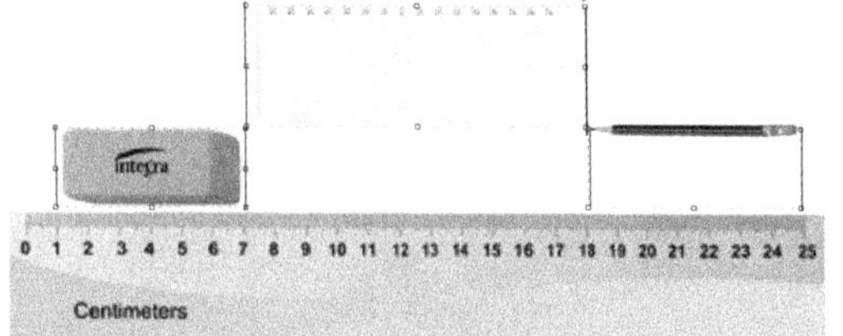 stands for 4 cars

39. There were __________ more cars parked on 3rd floor than on the 5th floor.
    (A) 4   (B) 16
    (C) 32   (D) 12

40. An ice cube resemble which geometric shape?

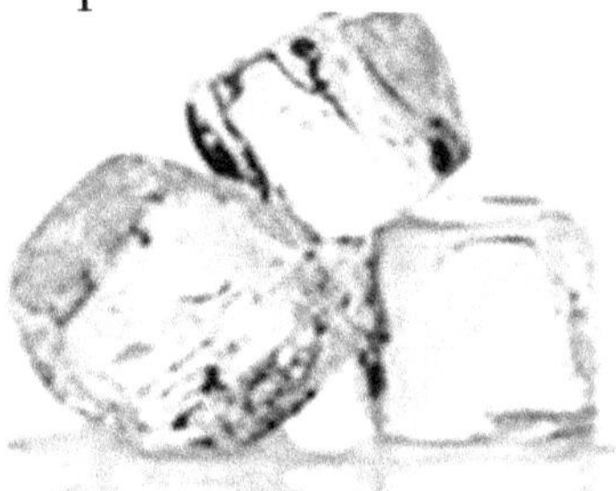

    (A) sphere   (B) circle
    (C) cube   (D) pyramid

Direction (41–44): Study the picture and answer the following questions.

41. The length of the eraser is __________ cm.
    (A) 7   (B) 6
    (C) 6.5   (D) 9

42. The length of the pencil is _______ cm.
   (A) 6
   (B) 8
   (C) 7
   (D) 7.5

43. Eraser is _______ cm shorter than the pencil.
   (A) 1 cm
   (B) 3 cm
   (C) 2 cm
   (D) 0.5 cm

44. The length of the notebook is _____ cm.
   (A) 18
   (B) 11
   (C) 12
   (D) 13

45. Look at the figure carefully and answer the following question.

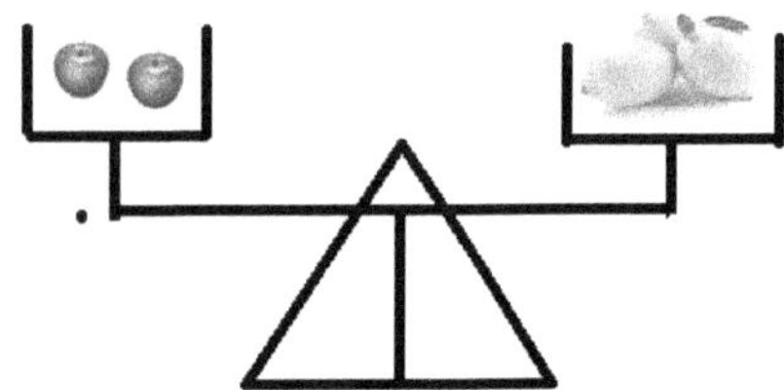

   If the weight of three apples is 250 grams, and all the three lemons are of same weight, then what is the weight of one lemon?
   (A) 75.55   (B) 73.33
   (C) 83.33   (D) 85.33

Direction: Select the correct option for each of the following questions.

46. The figure given below is made up of _________ triangles.

   (A) 5
   (B) 6
   (C) 7
   (D) 8

47. Which two shapes form the given figure?

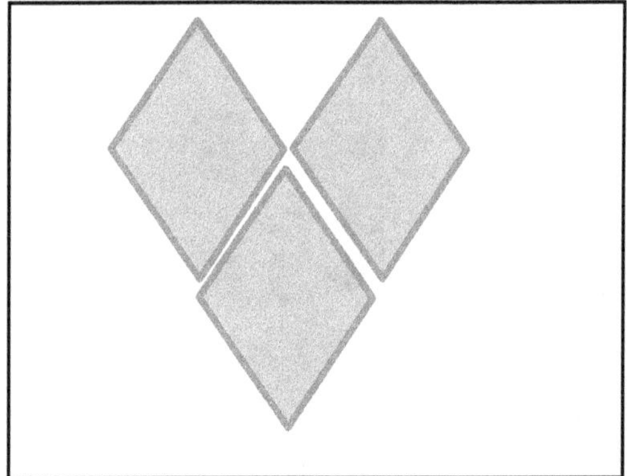

   (A) rhombus and square
   (B) triangle and square
   (C) kite and rhombus
   (D) rectangle and triangle

48. Which two types of geometrical shapes are hidden in the given picture?

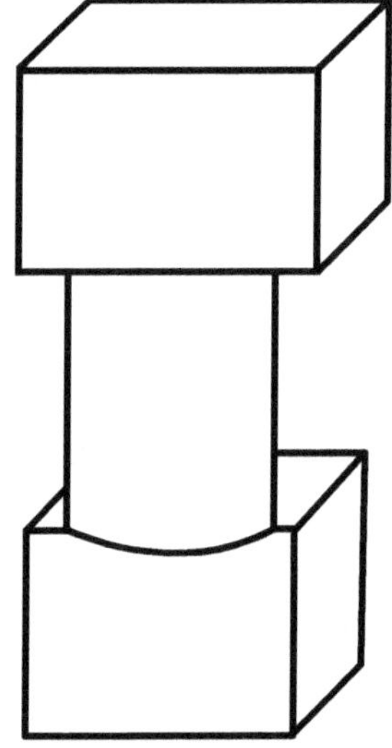

   (A) Square and cylinder
   (B) Rectangle and cylinder
   (C) Cubes and cylinder
   (D) Rectangle and cubes

49. How many lines are not straight lines in the given figure?

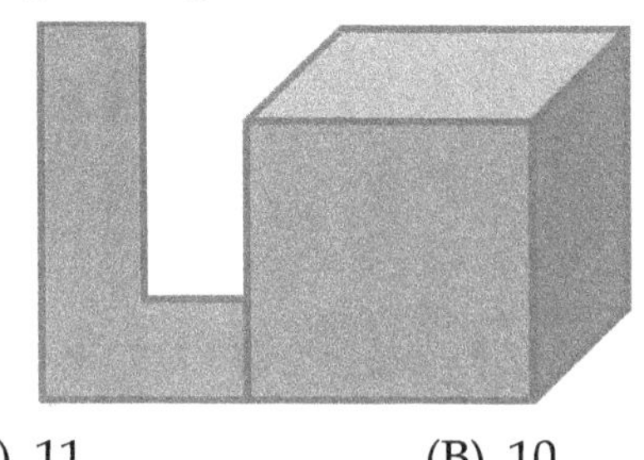

(A) 11   (B) 10
(C) 9   (D) 3

50. How many circles are there in the given face?

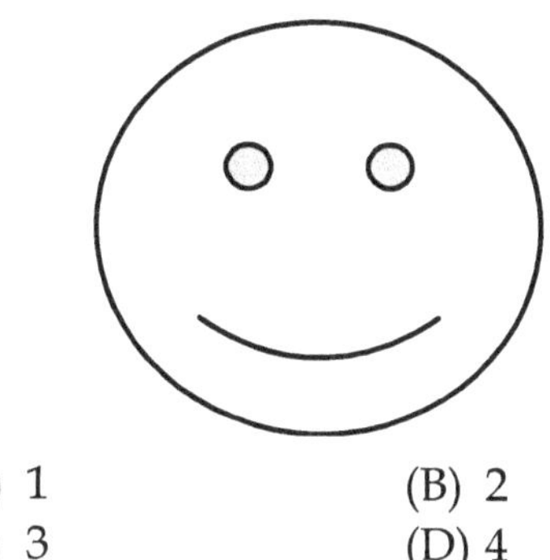

(A) 1   (B) 2
(C) 3   (D) 4

Darken Your Choice with HB Pencil

1.	A B C D	11.	A B C D	21.	A B C D	31	A B C D	41.	A B C D
2.	A B C D	12.	A B C D	22.	A B C D	32.	A B C D	42.	A B C D
3.	A B C D	13.	A B C D	23.	A B C D	33.	A B C D	43.	A B C D
4.	A B C D	14.	A B C D	24.	A B C D	34.	A B C D	44.	A B C D
5.	A B C D	15.	A B C D	25.	A B C D	35.	A B C D	45.	A B C D
6.	A B C D	16.	A B C D	26.	A B C D	36.	A B C D	46.	A B C D
7.	A B C D	17.	A B C D	27.	A B C D	37.	A B C D	47.	A B C D
8.	A B C D	18.	A B C D	28.	A B C D	38.	A B C D	48.	A B C D
9.	A B C D	19.	A B C D	29.	A B C D	39.	A B C D	49.	A B C D
10.	A B C D	20.	A B C D	30.	A B C D	40.	A B C D	50.	A B C D

MODEL TEST PAPER

MULTIPLE CHOICE QUESTIONS

1. Careful is to cautious as boastful is to________
   (A) arrogant   (B) humble
   (C) joyful   (D) suspicious

2. Look at this series: 80, 10, 70, 15, 60, ... What number should come next?
   (A) 20   (B) 25
   (C) 30   (D) 50

3. Look at this series: 8, 6, 9, 23, 87 , ... What number should come next?
   (A) 128   (B) 226
   (C) 324   (D) 429

Directions: The given word is followed by four answer choices. You have to choose the word that is a necessary part of the word.

4. School
   (A) student   (B) report card
   (C) test   (D) learning

Directions: Identify the letter pattern and number pattern and fill the blank in the middle of the series or end of the series.

5. JAK, KBL, LCM, MDN, _____
   (A) OEP   (B) NEO
   (C) MEN   (D) PFQ

6. Look at the following food chains. Write the correct word in the box.

   Leaf, tadpole, human

   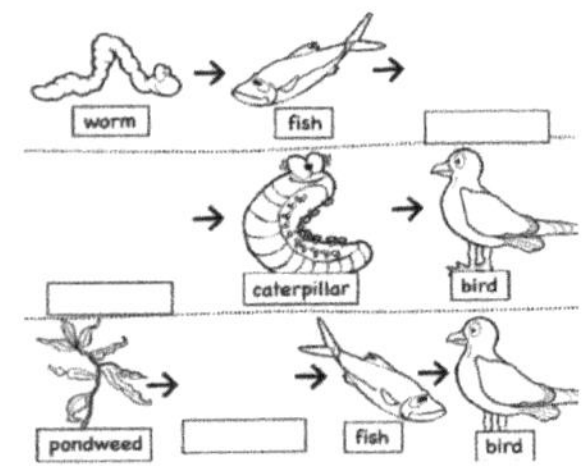

   (A) Human, leaf, tadpole
   (B) Tadpole, human, leaf
   (C) Leaf, human, tadpole
   (D) Leaf, tadpole, human

7. Classify the animals according to their external features:

   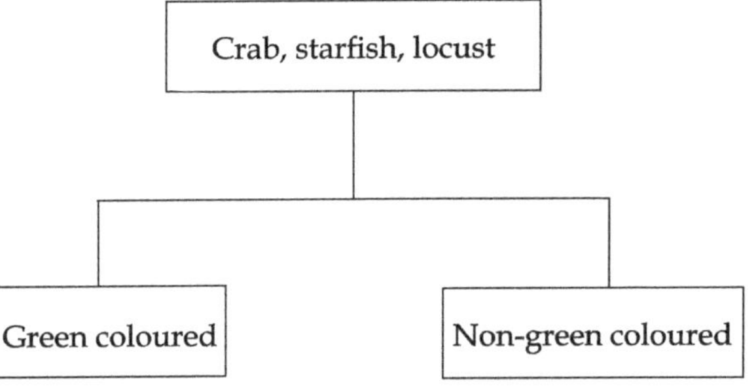

   (A) Locust, crab, starfish
   (B) Starfish, locust, crab
   (C) Crab, starfish, locust
   (D) Both (A) and (B)

8. Which of the following is not a plant?

   (A)    (B) 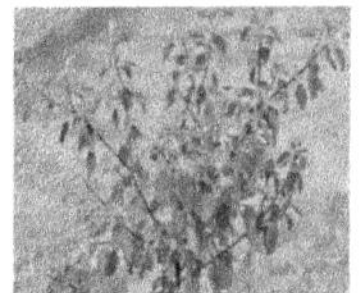

   (C)    (D) 

9. Which medicine is prepared by the trunk (bark) of a plant and used to cure malaria?

OLYMPIAD WORKBOOK (NSO) CLASS—2

(A) Cold syrup   (B) Quinine

(C) Cough syrup   (D) Penicillin

10. Look at the picture given below:

Can you list the parts of the body that help the deer escape from the lion?

(A) Ears, legs, heart

(B) Legs, eyes, ears

(C) Brain, eyes, legs

(D) Brain, heart, eyes

11. Which organ removes waste and water from the blood?

(A) 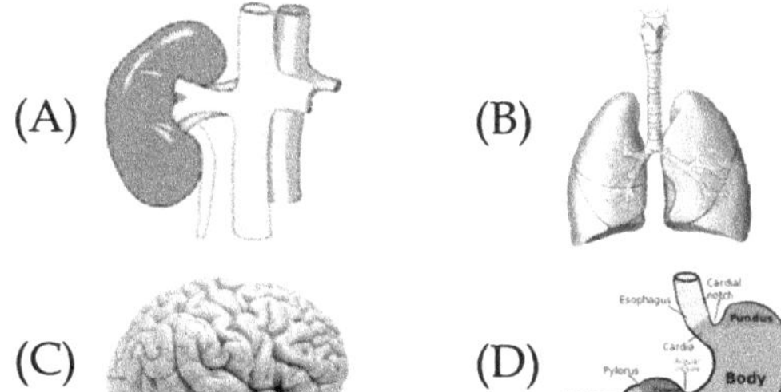 (B)

(C) (D)

12. Which of these foods give us energy?

(A) 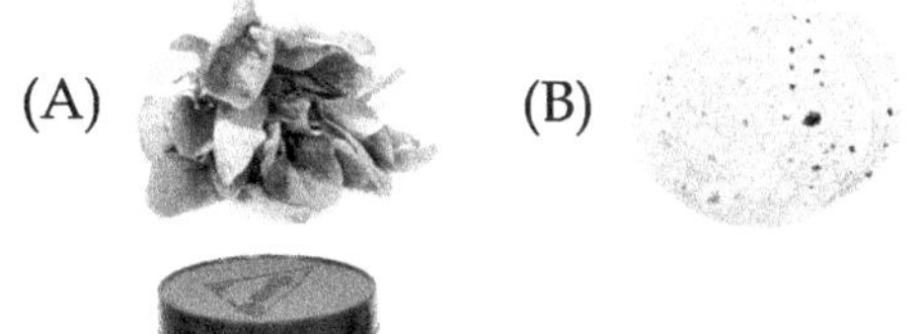 (B)

(C) (D) Both (B) and (C)

13. We need _______ to protect our body.

(A)  (B) 

(C) (D) All these

14. Which of these organs give us the sense of touch?

(A) Tongue   (B) Skin

(C) Ear   (D) Eye

15. Which of the following structures of a house can be flat, slopping, or semi-circular?

(A) Roof   (B) Floor

(C) Door   (D) Mud

16. Eskimos live in _________.

(A) Huts   (B) Caravans

(C) House boats   (D) Igloos

17. Observe the given image and identify the organism from which the following fibre is obtained _________.

(A) Worm   (B) Rabbit

(C) Snake   (D) Goat

18. Clothes are made from _________.

(A) Web   (B) Fibre

(C) Barks   (D) Microbes

19. Eid is celebrated every year as _________.

(A) Eid-ul-Zulha

(B) Eid-ul-Fitr

(C) Eid-ul-Milad

(D) All of these

20. Look at the following picture carefully. Which occasion in the Hindu family is shown in the picture?

(A) Housewarming
(B) Wedding
(C) Anniversary
(D) Birthday

21. Ananya is Gaurav's sister. Gaurav is Shruti's father. What will Shruti call Ananya?
(A) Aunt   (B) Sister
(C) Mother   (D) Sister-in-law

22. Potentially, a person is half similar to his/her ___________.
(A) Sibling   (B) Father
(C) Mother   (D) All of these

23. This person brings letters and parcels ___________.
(A) Nurse   (B) Postman
(C) Doctor   (D) Police

24. A musician does not use which of these items?

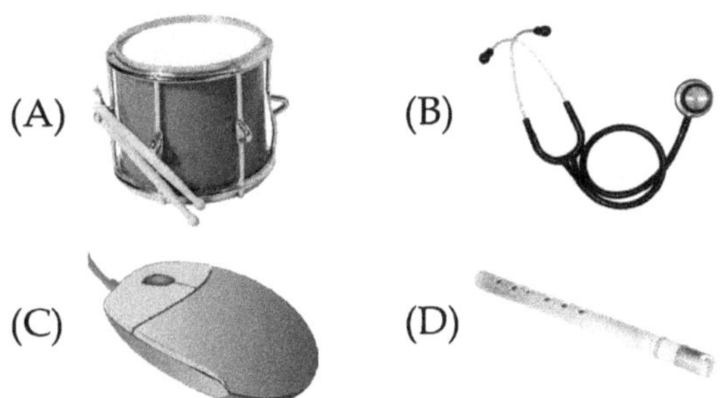

(A)   (B)

(C)   (D)

25. Which of the following is a wrong statement?
(A) Walk on the footpath.
(B) We must stand in a queue at the bus stop.
(C) Do not get in or out of the moving bus.
(D) Do not obey the traffic rules.

26. How many means of transport are hidden in the given word grid?

STRUCK
BUSCAR
OTRAIN
ISHIPO
UBOATF

(A) 4   (B) 5
(C) 6   (D) 7

27. In the following figure, what is Q?

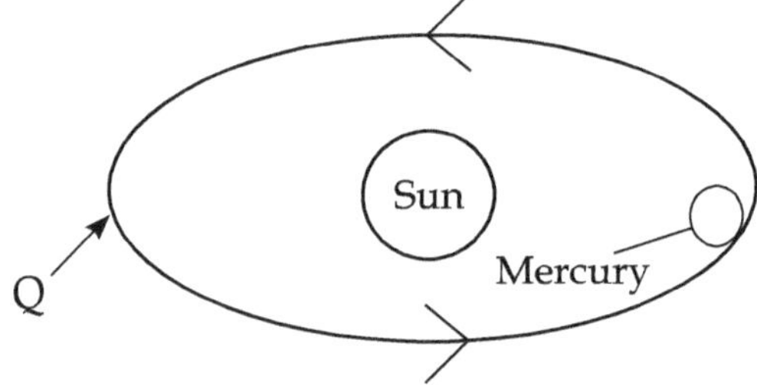

(A) Revolution   (B) Track
(C) Orbit   (D) Axis

28. A piece of land surrounded by water on three sides is called ___________.
(A) Continent
(B) Peninsula
(C) Island
(D) Plateau

29. Which of these colours is not found in the rainbow?
(A) Yellow   (B) Black
(C) Red   (D) Blue

OLYMPIAD WORKBOOK (NSO) CLASS–2

30. Match the columns and select the correct options.

I	II
A. Stomach	1. Pumps blood to all parts of the body
B. Brain	2. Helps us breathe
C. Lungs	3. Helps us in digestion
D. Heart	4. Helps us think and remember

(A) A-3; B-4; C-2; D-1

(B) A-2; B-1; C-4; D-3

(C) A-4; B-2; C-1; D-3

(D) A-2; B-4; C-3; D-1

31. Match column I with column II and select the correct options.

Column-I (Animal)	Column-II (Home)
A. Bee	1. Web
B. Rabbit	2. Stable
C. Spider	3. Kennel
D. Horse	4. Hive
E. Dog	5. Burrow

(A) A-1; B-2; C-3; D-4; E-5

(B) A-4; B-5; C-1; D-2; E-3

(C) A-1; B-5; C-3; D-4; E-2

(D) A-2; B-5; C-1; D-4; E-3

32. What is X and Y in the given rhyme about traffic signals?

> Twinkle, twinkle traffic light
> Shining on the corner bright.
> When it's 'X' it's time to go;
> When it's 'Z' it's time to STOP! you know.
> Twinkle, twinkle traffic light
> Shining on the corner bright.
> "Stop!" says the 'Z' light,
> "Go!" says the 'Y'.
> "Wait!" says the 'P',
> Till the light is 'X'.

	X	Y
A.	Red	Yellow
B.	Yellow	Red
C.	Green	Green

33. See the picture and guess what happens?

The following sentences tell a story, but they are in the wrong order. Write them in the correct order.

1. He fell into it.

2. He did not see the hole.

3. A bus stopped and an old man got off.

4. Yesterday some men dug a hole.

(A) 1, 2, 3, and 4

(B) 4, 1, 2, and 3

(C) 3, 2, 4, and 1

(D) 4, 3, 2, and 1

34. Look at the picture below carefully.

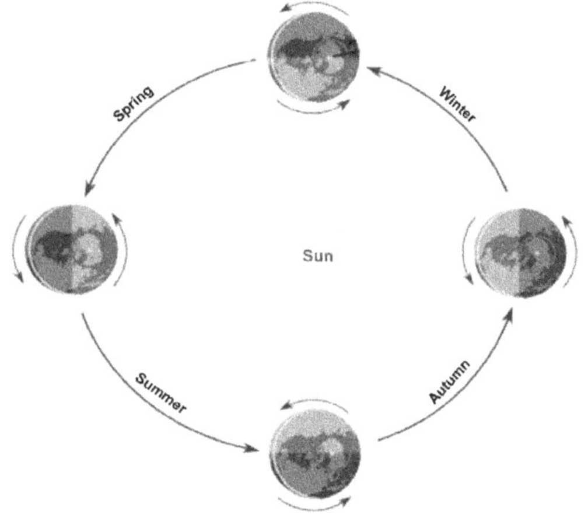

Now answer the following questions.

I. What causes the Sun to rise and set every day?

II. Which of these is most responsible for the changes of the seasons on Earth?

	I	II
(A)	Orbit of the Earth	Position of the Moon
(B)	Rotation of the Earth	Tilt of Earth on its axis
(C)	Revolution of the Earth	Temperature of the Sun
(D)	Rotation of the Earth	Rotation of the Earth

35. Air occupies space and has _________.
(A) Force
(B) Temperature
(C) Weight
(D) Both (A) and (B)

HINTS AND SOLUTIONS

1. PLANTS

Answer Key

1. (A)	2. (B)	3. (C)	4. (A)	5. (D)	6. (B)	7. (D)	8. (C)	9. (A)	10. (D)
11. (A)	12. (D)	13. (C)	14. (A)	15. (D)	16. (A)	17. (D)	18. (D)	19. (A)	20. (B)
21. (D)	22. (D)	23. (B)	24. (B)	25. (A)					

HOTS (ACHIEVERS SECTION)

26. (A)	27. (C)	28. (D)	29. (B)	30. (D)

2. ANIMALS

Answer Key

1. (A)	2. (C)	3. (D)	4. (D)	5. (B)	6. (D)	7. (B)	8. (A)	9. (B)	10. (D)
11. (B)	12. (C)	13. (D)	14. (A)	15. (D)	16. (C)	17. (C)	18. (B)	19. (D)	20. (A)
21. (D)	22. (A)	23. (C)	24. (D)	25. (B)					

HOTS (ACHIEVERS SECTION)

26. (A)	27. (B)	28. (A)	29. (C)	30. (B)

3. HUMAN BODY

Answer Key

1. (C)	2. (B)	3. (B)	4. (A)	5. (A)	6. (A)	7. (A)	8. (B)	9. (C)	10. (D)
11. (C)	12. (A)	13. (C)	14. (B)	15. (D)	16. (D)	17. (A)	18. (D)	19. (C)	20. (B)
21. (A)	22. (A)	23. (C)	24. (A)	25. (B)					

HOTS (ACHIEVERS SECTION)

26. (C)	27. (C)	28. (A)	29. (A)	30. (A)

4. FOOD

Answer Key

1. (A)	2. (C)	3. (C)	4. (A)	5. (B)	6. (A)	7. (D)	8. (B)	9. (C)	10. (D)
11. (B)	12. (B)	13. (B)	14. (C)	15. (A)	16. (A)	17. (C)	18. (D)	19. (C)	20. (C)
21. (C)	22. (C)	23. (A)	24. (D)	25. (D)					

HOTS (ACHIEVERS SECTION)

26. (B)	27. (C)	28. (C)	29. (B)	30. (B)

5. HOUSING AND CLOTHING

Answer Key

1. (C)	2. (D)	3. (B)	4. (C)	5. (B)	6. (D)	7. (D)	8. (C)	9. (B)	10. (A)
11. (B)	12. (B)	13. (C)	14. (C)	15. (A)	16. (B)	17. (D)	18. (D)	19. (C)	20. (B)
21. (D)	22. (D)	23. (B)	24. (C)	25. (B)					

HOTS (ACHIEVERS SECTION)

26. (C)	27. (B)	28. (D)	29. (C)	30. (B)

6. FAMILY AND FESTIVALS, OCCUPATIONS

Answer Key

1. (D)	2. (A)	3. (A)	4. (D)	5. (B)	6. (C)	7. (B)	8. (C)	9. (D)	10. (D)
11. (A)	12. (D)	13. (A)	14. (C)	15. (A)	16. (D)	17. (C)	18. (D)	19. (B)	20. (A)
21. (B)	22. (C)	23. (D)	24. (D)	25. (B)	26. (B)	27. (C)	28. (B)	29. (D)	30. (B)

HOTS (ACHIEVERS SECTION)

31. (B)	32. (A)	33. (D)	34. (D)	35. (C)

7. GOOD HABITS AND SAFETY RULES

Answer Key

1. (D)	2. (B)	3. (C)	4. (B)	5. (C)	6. (B)	7. (D)	8. (B)	9. (C)	10. (A)
11. (D)	12. (B)	13. (D)	14. (C)	15. (D)	16. (C)	17. (D)	18. (B)	19. (C)	20. (C)

OLYMPIAD WORKBOOK (NSO) CLASS – 2

1. (D)
We should take bath and brush everyday in the morning.
2. (B)
Taking bath daily is a good habit.
6. (B)
We use zebra crossing while crossing the road.

7. (D)
Wash you hands after bathing is NOT necessary.
8. (B)
At home we should never play with knife.
9. (C)
We should learn swimming with the help of an adult.

HOTS (ACHIEVERS SECTION)

21. (B)	22. (C)	23. (D)	24. (B)	25. (B)

22. (C)
A child should not go for swimming alone. As a beginner one should use swimming tube and swim with grown-up. Children should swim in the shallow end.

23. (D)

Dirt and germs collect in long nails and enter our mouth with food that we eat. Dirty hands also carry germs. These germs when enter our body, cause diseases. This is why Ramesh falls ill frequently in spite of taking healthy diet.

8. TRANSPORT AND COMMUNICATION

Answer Key

1. (B)	2. (A)	3. (B)	4. (D)	5. (D)	6. (D)	7. (B)	8. (C)	9. (C)	10. (D)
11. (A)	12. (A)	13. (D)	14. (D)	15. (A)	16. (A)	17. (D)	18. (A)	19. (B)	20. (B)
21. (C)	22. (C)	23. (D)	24. (B)	25. (A)					

HOTS (ACHIEVERS SECTION)

26. (A)	27. (D)	28. (A)	29. (C)	30. (B)

9. AIR, WATER AND ROCKS

Answer Key

1. (D)	2. (D)	3. (B)	4. (A)	5. (A)	6. (B)	7. (A)	8. (C)	9. (D)	10. (B)
11. (C)	12. (B)	13. (A)	14. (C)	15. (C)	16. (D)	17. (B)	18. (C)	19. (A)	20. (D)
21. (B)	22. (C)	23. (D)	24. (D)	25. (C)	26. (D)	27. (B)	28. (B)	29. (D)	30. (A)

HOTS (ACHIEVERS SECTION)

31. (C)	32. (C)	33. (C)	34. (A)	35. (B)

Answer Key

1. (A)	2. (A)	3. (C)	4. (B)	5. (B)	6. (A)	7. (D)	8. (C)	9. (A)	10. (D)
11. (B)	12. (D)	13. (C)	14. (B)	15. (B)	16. (B)	17. (C)	18. (C)	19. (D)	20. (B)
21. (D)	22. (C)	23. (C)	24. (A)	25. (A)					

HOTS (ACHIEVERS SECTION)

26. (B)	27. (B)	28. (A)	29. (A)	30. (B)

11. LOGICAL REASONING

Answer Key

1. (C)	2. (B)	3. (A)	4. (D)	5. (C)	6. (D)	7. (B)	8. (B)	9. (C)	10. (A)
11. (B)	12. (C)	13. (C)	14. (B)	15. (D)	16. (B)	17. (D)	18. (C)	19. (D)	20. (A)
21. (C)	22. (B)	23. (A)	24. (D)	25. (C)	26. (C)	27. (B)	28. (A)	29. (C)	30. (D)
31. (A)	32. (B)	33. (C)	34. (D)	35. (A)	36. (D)	37. (A)	38. (B)	39. (B)	40. (C)
41. (B)	42. (C)	43. (A)	44. (B)	45. (C)	46. (B)	47. (A)	48. (C)	49. (D)	50. (C)

1. (C)
   As Pen needs Ink to write; similarly Pencil needs Graphite.

2. (B)
   States with capital cities

3. (A)
   First figure rotates vertically downwards.

4. (D)
   Joining different parts to form a complete figure

5. (C)
   As mother is opposite to father; similarly grandmother is opposite to grandfather.

6. (D)
   $C(+1) \to D(+1) \to E(+1) \to F(+1) \to G(+1) \to H$

7. (B)
   $A(+3) \to D(+3) \to G(+3) \to J(+3) \to M(+3) \to P$

8. (B)
   $D(+2) \to F(+2) \to H(+2) \to J(+2) \to L(+2) \to N$

9. (C)
   $F(+1) \to G(+1) \to H(+1) \to I(+1) \to J(+1) \to K$

10. (A)
    $C(+2) \to E(+2) \to G(+2) \to I(+2) \to K(+2) \to M$

16. (B)
    Except (B) all the other options have a smaller shape inserted into a bigger shape.

17. (D)
    Add 4 to each number 4.

18. (C)
    Option (C) has six sides whereas shapes in the other options have four sides.

19. (D)

Option (D) is not a manually-played musical instrument.

20. (A)

(A) is healthy food whereas rest is all junk food.

21. (C)

As, T A B L E = 20 + 1 + 2 + 12 + 5 = 40

Similarly, C H A I R = 3 + 8 + 1 + 9 + 18 = 39

22. (B)

As, C A R R O T = 3 + 1 + 18 + 18 + 15 + 20 = 75

Similarly, R A D D I S H = 18 + 1 + 4 + 4 + 9 + 19 + 8 = 63

23. (A)

As, S E A = 19 − 5 − 1 = 13

Similarly, Y A K = 25 − 1 − 11 = 13

24. (D)

As, A = 1, B = 2, C = 3, D = 4 and so on.

Then, H = 8, E = 5, L = 12, P = 16

Similarly, H = 8, O = 15, R = 18, S = 19, E = 5

25. (C)

As, G = 7, O = 15, A = 1, T = 20

Similarly, S = 19, H = 8, E = 5, E = 5, P = 16

35. (A)

Here, every number comes after a gap of two numbers:

30 + 2 = 32

32 + 2 = 34

So, 34 + 2 = 36, 36 + 2 = 38 and 38 + 2 = 40

41. (B)

Eraser starting from 1 and ending at 7 cm, so length of the eraser

= 7 cm − 1 cm = 6 cm.

45. (C)

2 Apples = 3 lemons.

Weight of 2 apples = 250 grams, so weight of 3 lemons = 250 gm.

So, weight of 1 lemon = 250/3

= 83.33 gm.

MODEL TEST PAPER

Answer Key

1. (A)	2. (A)	3. (D)	4. (A)	5. (B)	6. (A)	7. (A)	8. (C)	9. (B)	10. (C)
11. (A)	12. (D)	13. (D)	14. (B)	15. (A)	16. (D)	17. (A)	18. (B)	19. (D)	20. (B)
21. (A)	22. (A)	23. (B)	24. (B)	25. (D)	26. (B)	27. (C)	28. (B)	29. (B)	30. (A)
31. (B)	32. (C)	33. (D)	34. (B)	35. (C)					

SAMPLE OMR ANSWER SHEET

1. STUDENT NAME (IN ENGLISH CAPITAL LETTERS ONLY)

Students must write and darken the respective circles completely using HB Pencil only. Othewise their Answer Sheets will not be evaluated.

PERSONAL DETAILS

2. SCHOOL CODE

3. CLASS

4. SECTION

5. ROLL NO.

6. QUESTION PAPER SET

- A ◯
- B ◯
- C ◯
- D ◯

7. MOBILE NUMBER

8. GENDER

MALE ◯
FEMALE ◯

9. STREAM
(Only for Class XI and XII Students)

MATHEMATICS ◯
BIOLOGY ◯
OTHERS ◯

MARK YOUR ANSWERS

1.	A B C D	26.	A B C D
2.	A B C D	27.	A B C D
3.	A B C D	28.	A B C D
4.	A B C D	29.	A B C D
5.	A B C D	30.	A B C D
6.	A B C D	31.	A B C D
7.	A B C D	32.	A B C D
8.	A B C D	33.	A B C D
9.	A B C D	34.	A B C D
10.	A B C D	35.	A B C D
11.	A B C D	36.	A B C D
12.	A B C D	37.	A B C D
13.	A B C D	38.	A B C D
14.	A B C D	39.	A B C D
15.	A B C D	40.	A B C D
16.	A B C D	41.	A B C D
17.	A B C D	42.	A B C D
18.	A B C D	43.	A B C D
19.	A B C D	44.	A B C D
20.	A B C D	45.	A B C D
21.	A B C D	46.	A B C D
22.	A B C D	47.	A B C D
23.	A B C D	48.	A B C D
24.	A B C D	49.	A B C D
25.	A B C D	50.	A B C D

Signature of the Student & Date of Examination

Signature of the Invigilator & Date of Examination

www.ingramcontent.com/pod-product-compliance
Lightning Source LLC
LaVergne TN
LVHW080438200726
843507LV00004B/853